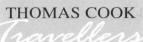

THOMAS COOK
Travellers

AMSTERDAM

AA

Produced by AA Publishing

Written by Christopher Catling

Series adviser: Melissa Shales

The Automobile Association would also like to thank:
Marjolein Schoe and Ellen Struik of Thomas Cook,
Amsterdam

Edited, designed and produced by AA Publishing. Maps ©
The Automobile Association 1993

Distributed in the United Kingdom by AA Publishing,
Fanum House, Basingstoke, Hampshire, RG21 2EA.

The contents of this publication are believed correct at the
time of printing. Nevertheless, the publishers cannot accept
responsibility for errors or omissions, or for changes in
details given. Assessments of attractions, hotels, restaurants
and so forth are based upon the author's own experience
and, therefore, descriptions given in this guide necessarily
contain an element of subjective opinion which may not
reflect the publishers' opinion or dictate a reader's own experiences on
another occasion.

**We have tried to ensure accuracy in this guide, but things do
change and we would be grateful if readers would advise us of any
inaccuracies they may encounter.**

A CIP catalogue record for this book is available from the British
Library.

ISBN 0 7495 0622 9

Published by The Automobile Association and the Thomas Cook
Group Ltd.

This book was produced using QuarkXPress™, Aldus Freehand™ and
Microsoft Word™ on Apple Macintosh™ computers.

Colour separation: BTB Colour Reproduction, Whitchurch,
Hampshire.

Printed by Edicoes ASA, Oporto, Portugal.

Cover picture: *Canal barge* (Inset: *Canal bus sign*)
Title page: *Amsterdam canal*
Above: *Dutch gable*

Contents

Introduction

Samuel Johnson said that anyone who tires of London must be weary of life itself. The same is true of Amsterdam, a seductive and entertaining city made all the more attractive by its manageable size and easy-going atmosphere. Amsterdam combines big city attractions with the character of an overgrown village. Packed into an area small enough to cross on foot in under half an hour are some 40 museums, over 60 theatres and 141 art galleries. The city is home to two internationally renowned orchestras as well as the Dutch national ballet and opera companies. Yet it has none of the stress, hype or tension of a big metropolis – bicycles are more numerous than cars, there are scores of congenial cafés where even first-time visitors are welcomed as old friends and – with the exception of brash Kalverstraat – you will search hard to find a supermarket or chain store; Amsterdammers far prefer their traditional corner-shop grocery stores and specialist retailers. Above all, Amsterdam is a lived-in city, not one devoted solely to tourism or commerce; after 5pm when businesses close for the day the streets throng with Amsterdammers, born and bred in the city, out for a walk or drinking with friends in pavement cafés, lending the city an almost Mediterranean atmosphere. Visitors to Amsterdam experience a living, vital city which Amsterdammers are proud to share – in the words of Nicolas Freeling, creator of the famous Dutch detective, Van der Valk, 'I know of no city where the outsider is so spontaneously taken to heart'.

Keizersgracht, one of Amsterdam's major canals

THOMAS COOK'S AMSTERDAM

Thomas Cook's first party to The Netherlands was organised in 1868. The following year he returned with a trip to the Amsterdam Exhibition. By 1899 Amsterdam was a regular feature of Cook's Tours. A brochure produced for that year advertised a conducted 'Easter tour to Holland and the Dead Cities of the Zuyder Zee', with first class hotels and second class travel, for £5 5s 0d. By then Thomas Cook had an office in Amsterdam at 83 Damrak. The 1911 brochure advertises a departure from London Liverpool Street at 8.30pm, travelling by Harwich and Hook of Holland to arrive at 7.30am the following day. Carriages were provided for a three-hour tour of the city, and excursions included the island of Marken, Broek ('the cleanest village in Holland' - it had at the time no roads leading to it, for fear that horses would foul the streets), Edam and Zaandam, where it was possible to see Peter the Great's cottage - still owned at the time by the Russian imperial family. One of the attractions of Amsterdam in Thomas Cook's lifetime was the opportunity for winter skating.

AMSTERDAM QUOTES

'Where else in the world could one choose a place where all life's commodities and all the curiosities one could wish for are so easy to find as here?'
René Descartes

'Heroic, Resolute, Compassionate'
The succinct motto on Amsterdam's coat of arms

'What impressed contemporaries about Amsterdam was that it was a city entirely dedicated to making money . . . all the way up the Damrak the quay was crammed with hoists, piles of merchandise, porters and small ships loading and unloading . . . almost the whole world seemed to be assembled to buy and sell.'
Mark Girouard

'I like to wander through the old narrow and rather sombre streets with their shops occupied by chemists, lithographers and ship's chandlers and browse among the navigation charts and other ship's supplies. I cannot tell you how beautiful the area is at twilight.'
Vincent van Gogh

'From my favourite spot on the floor I look up at the blue sky and the bare chestnut tree on whose branches little raindrops glisten like silver, and at the seagulls and other birds as they glide on the wind.'
Anne Frank

'The pungent salt smell, the northern, maritime keynotes of seagull and herring, the pointed brick buildings, tall and narrow like herons, with their mosaic of parti-coloured shutters, eaves, sills that give the landscape their stiff, heraldic look . . .'
Nicolas Freeling

'Amsterdam remains the refuge of all those striving to free themselves from the stifling atmosphere of small communities, and that too forms part of the city's strength and vitality.'
Geert Mak

History

1275
First documentary reference to 'Amstelledamme', meaning 'dam across the River Amstel'.

1300
Amsterdam gains its first municipal charter, enabling the town to create and enforce its own laws.

1323
Amsterdam gains a monopoly on the import of German beer. The town prospers on trade with England, Germany and the Baltic ports in grain, timber, cloth, furs, salt and fish.

1345
Pilgrims flock to Amsterdam after a communion host thrown into a fire is found intact in the embers and a miracle is declared.

1346
The city's oldest surviving convent, the Begijnhof, is founded.

1452
Fire destroys much of Amsterdam. New laws forbid the use of thatch and timber in favour of brick and tile.

1519
Charles V of Spain inherits Amsterdam as part of the Habsburg Empire. Though nominally a Catholic city, Amsterdam provides a refuge for persecuted Protestant minorities.

1535
Anabaptists riot in Amsterdam sparking a Catholic backlash.

1566
Calvinists storm Amsterdam's churches, winning the right to hold public services – an event known as the *Beeldenstorm*, the Iconoclasm.

1567
Philip II Of Spain, heir to Charles V, imposes strict Catholic rule on Amsterdam; Protestants are executed or flee to England.

1572
The Dutch revolt against Spanish rule begins under the leadership of William the Silent, Prince of Orange.

1578
Prince William's troops drive the Spanish from Amsterdam. Catholicism is outlawed and Calvinists take over city institutions, an event known as the *Alteratie*, the Alteration.

1579
The northern Dutch provinces sign the Treaty of Utrecht declaring their independence from Spain. Protestants expelled from Antwerp come to Amsterdam bringing skills that will pave the way for the Golden Age.

1595–7
Dutch expeditions discover navigable routes to Indonesia.

1602
The East India Company is set up to co-ordinate Dutch Far East trade.

1613
Work begins on the construction of the canal circle.

1621
The West India Company is set up to co-ordinate Dutch trade with the Americas and Africa.

1626
Peter Minuit founds New Amsterdam on the Hudson River.

1642
Rembrandt paints *The Night Watch*.

1650
Amsterdam is now the biggest Dutch city (population 220,000), and capital of a trading empire stretching from Australia to the Antilles.

1664
New Amsterdam is captured by the English and renamed New York.

1689
The Dutch prince, William III of Orange, is crowned King of England.

18th century
Amsterdam's maritime trade is slowly crippled by a series of costly wars.

1795
The Velvet Revolution; French revolutionary troops invade Amsterdam and are welcomed by reformers who establish a new National Assembly.

1806
Napoleon invades Amsterdam and sets his brother, Louis Napoleon, on the Dutch throne.

1813
The northern and southern provinces of The Netherlands are briefly united.

1831
The southern provinces declare their independence; the Kingdom of Belgium is born.

1845
Riots in Amsterdam lead to democratic reform and the establishment of a directly elected parliament under J R Thorbecke.

1848–76
Major improvements in housing, education and health. Amsterdam experiences a boom with the opening of the Nordzee Kanaal (North Sea Canal) and the discovery of new diamond fields in South Africa.

1914–18
Amsterdam remains neutral during World War I but suffers the effects of anti-German food blockades.

1928
The Olympic Games are held in Amsterdam.

1940
Nazis invade The Netherlands.

1942
Anne Frank and her family go into hiding.

1945
Amsterdam liberated from German occupation.

1949
The former Dutch colony of Indonesia wins independence.

1963
First squatter protests against Amsterdam's acute housing problem.

1965
Anarchistic 'Provocateurs' win seats on Amsterdam's city council.

1969
John Lennon and Yoko Ono stage their 'lie-in' peace protest at the Amsterdam Hilton.

1975
Riots over plans to demolish an area of Nieuwmarkt to build the Metro system and Stadhuis complex.

1982
Three days of rioting following the forcible eviction of squatters: a state of emergency is declared.

1983
Ed van Thijn is elected mayor and takes tough action against crime, drugs and squatters.

1989
New plans are devised to make Amsterdam traffic free.

1990
Amsterdam hosts the Van Gogh centenary exhibition and receives a record number of visitors.

Geography

*A*msterdam is the capital of The Netherlands, one of the smallest countries in Europe. The country measures approximately 257km north to south and 180km east to west, and it is divided into 12 provinces. English-speaking visitors often refer, incorrectly, to the country as Holland. Strictly speaking, Holland consists only of the two western provinces bordering the North Sea: Noord (North) Holland, in which Amsterdam is located (though Haarlem is the provincial capital), and Zuid (South) Holland (provincial capital, Den Haag, also known as The Hague and seat of the Dutch Government).

These two provinces, along with the province of Utrecht (capital, Utrecht) form a region known as the *Randstad,* meaning 'ring town', so called because its cities form an almost circular conurbation. It is also known, more affectionately, as 'the big village', and it has a population of over 4 million – 27 per cent of the Dutch total of 14.8 million.

The *Randstad* is economically prosperous, accounting for almost half the country's total output. Amsterdam itself is an important banking and financial services centre. Around a third of the city's income comes from small businesses and the self-employed. Despite its laid-back atmosphere, the city is a hive of entrepreneurship, with many people employed in computer consultancy, graphic design, journalism,

Deltawerken: the sea dominates the geography and the history of The Netherlands

publishing, architecture and the arts. Tourism and retailing are also major sources of revenue and employment.

The other cities of the *Randstad* include Rotterdam, the world's biggest port, Delft, Leiden and Gouda. Schiphol airport is also critical to the *Randstad* economy. Most visitors see it only as an efficient passenger airport but behind the scenes it has a huge freight-handling capacity and is a major distribution hub for European exports and imports – especially perishable goods, such as fruit, vegetables and cut flowers. Many of the exotic and out-of-season fruits that fill European supermarket shelves are flown in to Schiphol from the Far East, Africa, the Caribbean and the Canary Islands for onward distribution by road.

This in turn has benefited the Dutch horticultural and agricultural industries. Much of the land to the south and west of Amsterdam is used for growing flowers, pot plants and greenhouse fruit and vegetables, such as tomatoes, peppers, cucumbers and strawberries. Tulip bulbs are the most famous product of the region but in terms of sales they actually rank fourth behind roses, chrysanthemums and carnations. The bulb fields and gardens around Lisse, just south of Amsterdam, are a major tourist attraction in their own right, as is the world's largest daily flower auction at Aalsmeer, adjacent to Schiphol airport.

Much of the land around Amsterdam has been reclaimed over the centuries by constructing a complex system of dykes and dams to hold back the sea and drain the watery landscape. The resulting land is called polder, from *pol,* referring to the wooden poles or stakes that were originally used to stabilise the sides of the drainage dykes. Wind-powered mills were once used to raise the water

A land reclaimed from the sea

through a series of ring canals, each one higher than the last, so that the water could eventually flow via natural rivers out to the sea. Nowadays the task of drainage is handled by electric pumps, but well-preserved windmills are still a characteristic feature of the Dutch landscape especially to the north of Amsterdam, around Zaanse Schans.

The most recent area of polderisation lies immediately to the east of Amsterdam. The shallow IJsselmeer (formerly known as the Zuider Zee) was dammed in 1932 by building the 30km Afsluitdijk (Enclosing Dike). Part of the IJsselmeer was then drained to create Flevoland; this huge area of reclaimed land, measuring 1,800sq km, was officially declared the 12th province of The Netherlands in 1986. Today such large-scale polderisation schemes are surrounded by controversy. Environmentalists fear that further drainage of the IJsselmeer would damage a fragile ecology. Furthermore, if the water table falls below its present level the wooden piles supporting Amsterdam's older buildings might dry out and rot, causing damage on a massive scale. To the relief of Amsterdam residents, further schemes have been put on hold and a temporary truce has been drawn in the elemental battle between the land and the sea.

Politics

*T*he Netherlands has a three-tier system of government with a national parliament based in Den Haag (The Hague) responsible for defence, overall fiscal policy and foreign affairs; provincial councils, based in each of the 12 provincial capitals, are responsible for managing the local infrastructure and city councils are responsible for running the large municipalities. The system is highly devolved and the Amsterdam city council has a very wide range of powers and responsibilities, while national politics has very little impact on the city. In recent years the council has had to face an awesome range of issues, and it has developed progressive, though not always successful, policies to manage the problems of housing, unemployment, race relations, inner-city renewal, drugs and crime.

In the 1970s, what had hitherto been a series of relatively peaceful protests turned violent. On 'Blue Monday', 24 March 1975, police and protesters battled in the streets over plans to demolish an area of Nieuwmarkt to build the new Stadhuis or City Hall. In 1982 a state of emergency was declared after police attempts to evict squatters sparked off three days of rioting. Amsterdam was seen as one of the most troubled cities in Europe.

Today the anarchy of previous decades has given way to hard-headed pragmatism, tempered by traditional Dutch humanism. In 1983 Ed van Thijn was elected mayor of the 45-member city council and set about resolving the problems of housing, drugs, petty crime and general economic decline.

Various experiments have been tried to tackle the drugs problem. Initially, non-Dutch addicts were deported and the remainder were given free heroin in an attempt to stamp out illegal dealing and petty crime. This proved unsuccessful and the authorities have now placed their hopes in a programme of medical help for heroin addicts, whose numbers have now stabilised.

On the housing front, the squatter movement had one lasting effect; the wholesale clearance of 'slum' areas has been halted in favour of sympathetic small-scale regeneration. The city owns 40 per cent of the housing stock and 70 per cent of the land; its policy now is to lease this to developers who build new apartments or restore old buildings for rent. Critics claim that rents have soared

The World Trade Centre in Amsterdam

The Houses of Parliament, seat of the Dutch government

as a result, and there are long waiting lists for attractive canal-side flats.

On the other hand, problems remain beyond the city centre. Amsterdam has a large ethnic community; around 25 per cent of the city's 700,000 population are of Turkish or Moroccan origin. Many were brought in as 'guest workers' in the 1960s, others derive from former Dutch colonies – the Antilles, Surinam and Indonesia. Many live in soulless tower blocks on estates such as Bijlmermeer, in the south of the city. Ironically, these flats, designed on the futuristic principles of Le Corbusier, were originally built as luxury apartments, but their intended occupants preferred to stay put in the city centre rather than live in an alienating suburban environment.

Part of the answer has been to redevelop Bijlmermeer, replacing the tower blocks with new housing on a more human scale. Businesses have been encouraged to open up here as well to provide much-needed local employment.

Amsterdam's problems have been made worse by the closure of several big industrial enterprises, such as the former shipyards. Other businesses have moved, many to Rotterdam. Heineken's decision to relocate to Zouterwoude in 1986 was a further blow, even though residents had often complained about the smell of the brewery and its massive trucks clogging up the city's narrow roads.

In response to the threat of decline and unemployment, a huge regeneration scheme is now planned for the redundant docklands area which stretches for 15km behind Amsterdam Centraal station. It is hoped that multinational companies will establish headquarters here from which to take advantage of the post-1992 single European market.

In a complex city like Amsterdam it is difficult to find political solutions that please everyone, yet much has been achieved since the stormy days of the 1970s. Slowly but surely the city council is achieving its objective of *stadsvernieuwing* – urban renewal; instead of ending up a ghost town or a gigantic tourist theme park, Amsterdam remains an invigorating, cultural and energetic city that Amsterdammers genuinely like to live in.

Culture

*A*msterdam has its own distinctive culture which embraces the extremes of tradition and the avant-garde. On the one hand Amsterdammers are wedded to the old-world charm of brown cafés lit by *schemerlampen*, twilight lamps that cast a golden glow. Crowds gather round street-side herring stalls in spring to sample the mild *nieuwe haring*, the first of the season, while all over the city bright ornate barrel-organs pump out old-fashioned fairground music.

On the other hand this is a city that loves the experimental. Theatres mount productions in which the cast consists entirely of barking Alsatian dogs. Galleries host 'events' where participants transform each other into living works of art by daubing their naked bodies with paint. Amsterdam could never be accused of dreariness.

Such contradictions are part of the cultural diversity of a city which sometimes seems obsessed by art – not surprising when you consider how many Amsterdammers make their living in architecture, design, photography, journalism and other creative professions. Sometimes passions run out of control. *The Night Watch* has been attacked with knives and acid on several occasions by frustrated individuals,

Everywhere something to delight the eye

envious that their own work does not attract as much attention as Rembrandt's masterpiece.

Such extreme gestures are hardly justified in a city that offers so many outlets for creative expression. The arts are encouraged by the 'One Per Cent Rule' whereby one per cent of the capital cost of any new building in the city is set aside to fund public murals, paintings or sculpture. The city's streets are awash with performers: Dam square, Leidseplein, Stationsplein and Vondelpark throng with buskers in summer and punk rockers, acrobats and puppeteers compete for attention with bongo players and mime artists. Many of the city's buses and trams have been turned into mobile works of art by students of the Rietvald Academy. Even shopkeepers and homeowners enter into the spirit of artistic endeavour; the shopping streets of Jordaan and the canal circle are enlivened by eye-catching window displays and the owners of smart canal-side apartments leave their curtains open at night to reveal tasteful interiors – every item of furniture, every

In the warm glow of a brown café

plant and picture carefully chosen to make a statement to any passers-by.

Several times a year Amsterdammers come together for big street festivals; for Queen's Day, Koninginnedag (30 April), for carnival, for the Jordaan festival in early September and for the Aalsmeer to Amsterdam floral parade at the end of the month. Here again Amsterdam reveals its love of extremes. Traditional accordion players and oompah bands alternate with heavy rock and experimental jazz bands to entertain the crowds on makeshift stages set up in front of street cafes. Everyone wears fancy dress, ranging from the freakish to the chic. All heads turn at the arrival of a popular character known simply as Fabiola, whose outlandish and inventive costumes have become part of Amsterdam folklore. Further style is added by the ethnic costumes worn by the large number of Caribbean, Surinamese and Indonesian participants.

Two further set-piece events attract festive crowds. In June some of the

world's top performers come together for the month-long Holland Festival. In August, theatre, dance and music companies from all over The Netherlands perform extracts from the year's forthcoming programme in the streets of Amsterdam. This event, called the *Uitmarkt*, is a huge open-air arts market designed to sell advance tickets; for the visitor it provides an opportunity to sample the complete spectrum of the arts, from the conventional to the way-out fringe. During the rest of the year the cultural calendar is crowded with events: opera and ballet at the Muziektheater, concerts by the world-renowned Royal Concertgebouw Orchestra (under Riccardo Chailly) or The Netherlands Philharmonic, jazz at the BIMHuis, world music at the Melkweg (Milky Way), rock concerts at Paradiso, not to mention scores of events hosted by small clubs and arts cafés. Amsterdam is famed for its tolerance, its live and let live philosophy, and in that atmosphere, cultural pluralism thrives – there is no taste, no matter how traditional or way out, that is not catered for.

Finding your feet

*T*he historic heart of Amsterdam is very compact and can be crossed on foot in under half an hour. Trams, departing from Amsterdam Centraal station, reach all parts of the city and there is a Museumboat service which circles the canal system every 45 minutes calling at landing stages close to the major museums (for further details see Public Transport in the **Practical Guide**).

Even so, the best way to get to know the city is to walk. If you take to the streets in comfortable shoes, you will be rewarded by glimpses of Amsterdam at work and play and discover the rich diversity of the city's architecture. Enticing shops selling flowers, crafts, antiques or books, will arrest your attention and when you are tired you can be sure there is a pavement café, serving coffee or *warme chokolade* topped with whipped cream, waiting just around the corner.

Another way to gain a swift overview of the city is to take a canal cruise; knowledgeable guides will point out the key buildings and features and, seen from the water as it was intended to be, Amsterdam takes on a whole new perspective.

A canal cruise is a must for visitors

The canals frozen over in 1644

AMSTERDAM AREA BY AREA

When viewed on a map, Amsterdam has a distinctive shape; its several districts lock together like pieces in a jigsaw, and they represent separate phases in the deliberately planned development of the city. Once you understand the city's layout you will find it easier to negotiate the cobweb-like pattern of canals, streets and squares.

The Medieval City

Nearly everyone receives their first glimpse of Amsterdam from Centraal station, the arrival point of trains from the airport and from all over Europe. The station stands on the site of the original harbour which was partly filled in during the 19th century. From Stationsplein, which is usually crowded with buskers and commuters, the city's main street – Damrak – leads to the main square. This is simply called Dam and, as the name suggests, it is built over the site of the original dam across the River Amstel, after which the city was named. This dam probably had lock gates, allowing small craft to pass through and was designed to control the tidal flow of the river. Two of the city's most imposing buildings stand on the right-hand (western) side of the square: the Koninklijk Paleis (Royal Palace) and the Nieuwe Kerk (New Church).

Damrak runs through the heart of the oldest part of Amsterdam, dividing it into two parts which, on the map, look like a pair of lungs. To the east (left, with your back to the station) is the Oude Zijd (OZ), or Old Side, district, which was already built up by the 13th century. To the west is the slightly younger Nieuwe Zijd (NZ), New Side, district, first developed in the 14th century.

Medieval Amsterdam was surrounded by a defensive rampart. This has since disappeared but its position is indicated by the names of Oudezijds Voorburgwal and Oudezijds Achterburgwal meaning, respectively, in front of and behind the city wall. These two canals themselves started out as defensive moats. Their counterparts to the west, Nieuwezijds Voorburgwal and Achterburgwal, have since been filled in.

The Royal Palace on Dam square

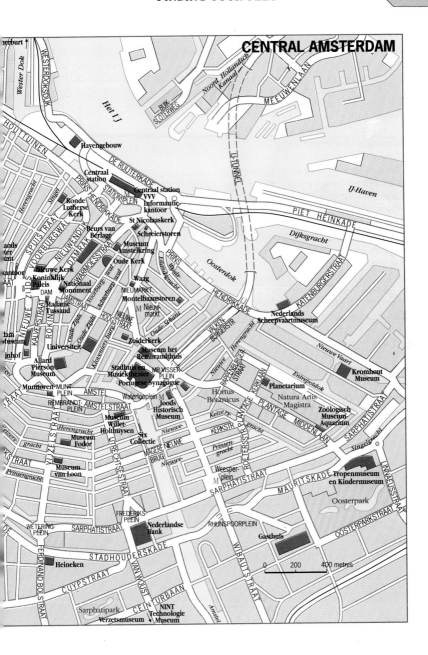

CENTRAL AMSTERDAM

Iterburt

Wester Dok

Het IJ

WESTERDOKSDIJK

HOUTTUINEN

Noord Hollandsch Kanaal

RIJK SOTERWEG

MEEUWENLAAN

DE RUIJTERKADE

IJ-Haven

Hayengebouw

PIET HEINKADE

Centraal station

STATIONSPLEIN

Centraal station
VVV Informatie-kantoor

St Nicolaaskerk

Dijksgracht

Ronde Luthurse Kerk

PRINS HENDRIKKADE

Beurs van Berlage

Schreierstoren

Oosterdok

Museum Amstelkring

Oude Kerk

Nieuwe Kerk

Koninklijk Paleis

Nationaal Monument

Waag

NIEUMARKT

Montelbaanstoren

M Nieuw markt

HENDRIKKADE

KATENBURGERSTRAAT

Nederlands Scheepvaartmuseum

Madame Tussaud

HOOGSTRAAT

Nieuwe Vaart

Zuiderkerk

Universiteit

Allard Pierson Museum

Museum het Rembrandthuis

Stadhuis en Muziektheater

MR VISSER PLEIN

Entrepotdok

Kromhout Museum

Portugese Synagogue

Planetarium

Munttoren MUNT PLEIN

AMSTEL

Waterlooplein

Hortus Botanicus

Natura Artis Magistra

REMBRANDT PLEIN

AMSTELSTRAAT

Joods Historisch Museum

Zoölogisch Museum-Aquarium

Museum Willet-Holthuysen

Museum Fodor

Six Collectie

Nieuwe.

MAGERE NIEUWE BRUG

Prinsen-gracht

Museum van Loon

Weesper Mplein

SARPHATISTRAAT

Tropenmuseum en Kindermuseum

Oosterpark

FREDERIKS PLEIN

Nederlandse Bank

RHIJNSPOORPLEIN

OOSTERPARKSTRAAT

WETERING PLEIN

SARPHATISTRAAT

Gasthuis

Heineken

STADHOUDERSKADE

0   200   400 metres

CUYPSTRAAT

CEINTURBAAN

Sarphatipark

NINT Technologie Museum

Verzetsmuseum

The Canal Circle

Wrapped around the core of the medieval city is the Grachtengordel, the canal circle, consisting of three concentric canals built in the 17th century and the main focus of architectural interest in the city. The harbour end of the canal circle, around Brouwersgracht, was the first to be developed, beginning in 1613. As building progressed the houses became ever grander; the point in the canal furthest from the harbour is known as the Golden Bend because of the wealth of its former inhabitants and the palatial splendour of their houses, many of which now serve as bank premises and embassies.

The Museum Quarter

Immediately adjacent to the Golden Bend is the Museum Quarter, a wedge-shaped block built as an extension to the city in the 19th century. Here you will find the famous Rijksmuseum and Van Gogh Museum, as well as the Stedelijk Museum of Modern Art. Behind the Museum Quarter is Vondelpark, scene of open-air concerts in summer, and the Concertgebouw, famed for its orchestra and excellent acoustics.

A short way further out is the district called De Pijp (The Pipe) because of its long, narrow tunnel-like streets. The principal thoroughfare, Albert Cuypstraat, hosts a bustling and colourful street market where it is possible to buy just about anything. The street is also renowned for its inexpensive ethnic restaurants and the diamond business of A van Moppes & Zoon.

The Museum Quarter is linked to the city centre by Nieuwe Spiegelstraat, which has the biggest concentration of

antique shops in Amsterdam and makes for fascinating browsing. The canal circle continues round from here until it is interrupted by the River Amstel. It then continues for a short way on the opposite

GREATER AMSTERDAM

bank to meet the district known as Plantage. As the name suggests this is a leafy suburb which was originally laid out as a pleasure garden; by the late 18th century wealthy businessmen began to build country houses here, but several large green spaces remain, such as the zoo (known as Artis Magister) and the Hortus Botanicus (Botanical Gardens).

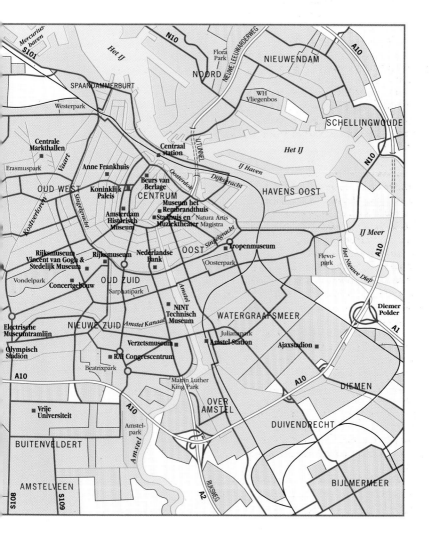

The Jewish Quarter

Coming back towards the city centre, the next district is Jodenbuurt, the former Jewish Quarter, with its synagogues, the Jewish Historical Museum and the Rembrandthuis (Rembrandt's House) Museum. Jodenbuurt has been comprehensively redeveloped since World War II and has a character entirely different to the rest of central Amsterdam, dominated as it is by the controversial new Stadhuis (City Hall) and the Muziektheater complex, home to the Netherlands Opera and National Ballet.

The familiar Amsterdam of characterful canals and old houses returns as you cross from Jodenbuurt into Nieuwmarkt, a district of great contrasts. To the south is the attractive maze of buildings that form the university, while to the north, around Zeedijk, is the red-light district and Chinatown.

A city that respects the individual

The Magere Brug or 'Skinny Bridge'

Amsterdam has several other districts of note. The eastern harbour, adjacent to Plantage and Jodenbuurt, has numerous old warehouses recently converted to apartments, and the excellent Nederlands Scheepvaart (Dutch Maritime) Museum. On the other side of the city, Jordaan (from the French *jardin,* garden) was, despite its name, an industrial suburb of narrow lanes and cramped workshops. Today it is a characterful neighbourhood of craft and speciality shops and ethnic restaurants.

THE CHARACTER OF AMSTERDAM

Amsterdam is an overgrown village, a comfortable congenial city whose relaxed pace is symbolised by the lumbering old-fashioned bicycles adopted by many residents for getting about, or the barges that make their sedate progress along the city's numerous canals.

At the same time there are aspects to the city that may puzzle or shock the first-time visitor. Ugly graffiti disfigures many fine buildings and the streets are slippery with dog faeces. Dishevelled drug addicts loiter around the station,

Prostitutes overtly plying their trade

'smoking bars' openly serve marijuana-laced cigarettes or cakes and prostitutes operate in full public view from sitting rooms lit by red neon.

This side of Amsterdam reflects the city's live and let live attitude, a philosophical outlook whose pluses and minuses are a frequent topic of debate amongst Amsterdammers themselves. Fundamentally, Amsterdammers value freedom from interference – whether from neighbours or officialdom. In their respect for privacy they turn a blind eye to what others choose to do, even to the anti-social behaviour of middle-class dog owners and rebellious adolescents with spray cans.

As a result, Amsterdam has a tolerant, permissive culture, but one that has been exploited by the unscrupulous few, including the drug dealers and pornographers who have tarnished the city's image. This casts a shadow over what local people consider real achievements, such as racial harmony, the espousal of gay rights and of sexual equality.

Amsterdammers will talk about such issues with humour and frankness; one of the delights of the city is the ease with which people engage in conversation, even with total strangers. They have the linguistic skills to do so; 70 per cent of the city's population speaks English and many also speak French and German. The Dutch educational system encourages language learning from an early age and Amsterdammers remain linguistically adroit by watching or listening to European TV and radio; many prefer the output of the British BBC to that of their own rather stolid national broadcasting authority.

They also read voraciously – Amsterdam is one of Europe's largest markets for books and shelves full of well-thumbed volumes in several languages are an essential part of the furnishings in any self-respecting city home. Central to all this is one overriding characteristic: respect for the quality of life. Amsterdammers are entrepreneurial but not workaholic; furthering their careers is less important than family life, time spent with friends or a visit to the theatre. Many visitors find that this refreshing and admirable attitude is highly infectious.

Lido Casino on Singelgracht

Just one of many second-hand bookstores

Bicycles

The bicycle is Amsterdam's favourite mode of transport – there are 550,000 bikes in a city of 700,000 people, many of them painted with colourful designs and transformed into minor works of art. The White Bikes scheme of 1966 was intended to provide free cycles for everyone; the scheme foundered in days when all the bikes were stolen, repainted and sold.

Placenames

To find your way about Amsterdam it helps to know that **plein** means square, **straat** street, **kerk** church, **huis** house and **gracht** canal. The three main canals are Herengracht (the Gentlemen's Canal), Keizersgracht (the Emperor's Canal, named after the Holy Roman Emperor, Maximilian I) and Prinsengracht (Prince's Canal, named after Prince William of Orange who liberated the city from Spanish rule).

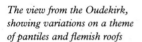

*The view from the Oudekirk,
showing variations on a theme
of pantiles and flemish roofs*

*The Northern Church painted in
1644 by Abraham Beerstraten*

*Though there have been some modern and inelegant
encroachments, the roofscape of Amsterdam remains
remarkably intact and unspoiled*

The Grachtengordel

Amsterdam's remarkable Grachtengordel, or canal ring, represents one of the earliest examples of deliberate town planning in Europe. The scheme was devised by Hendrik Staets, the municipal carpenter, in 1609. His plan for the controlled expansion of the city has an elegant logic. Three new canals were dug, the Herengracht, Keizersgracht and Prinsengracht, with a combined length of 12km. Each canal is 25m wide, broad enough to accommodate four lanes of barges or lighters, the small, shallow-draughted boats used to unload cargo from bigger ships moored in the harbour. Up to 4,000 boats could be accommodated and 17th-century engravings show the canal circle as a forest of masts, its wide, tree-shaded quays bustling with porters.

Housing plots were sold to merchants with precisely 30m of frontage, though some variation can be detected amongst the general uniformity; sometimes property speculators bought up two adjoining plots and resold them as one, enabling palatial residences to be built, or they subdivided them into three narrower plots.

Planning laws stipulated the maximum depth of houses to ensure a degree of space and light between houses backing onto each other on adjacent canals. This garden space was, in some cases, built over at a later date to provide an *achterhuis,* a back annexe, such as the one in which Anne Frank and her family hid from Nazi persecution. Even so, the canal circle still has numerous hidden gardens, as anyone who climbs the tower of Westerkerk will discover.

Shops were only permitted on the narrow interlinking radial canals, which is where they are still found to this day. This policy ensured that the three principal canals present an unbroken vista of houses, individualised by ornate gables and cornices, sculptural reliefs and fine doorcases; spotting the endless variations is one of the great pleasures of a leisurely stroll around this most elegant of cities.

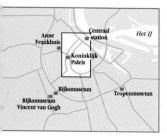

Central Amsterdam

This walk covers the main sights of the city centre and is intended to help you gain your bearings. *Allow 1 hour*

Start at Amsterdam Centraal station

1 AMSTERDAM CENTRAAL

Amsterdam's palatial railway station was built in 1889 by P J H Cuypers, the same architect who designed the Rijksmuseum. Around 100,000 travellers pass through it every

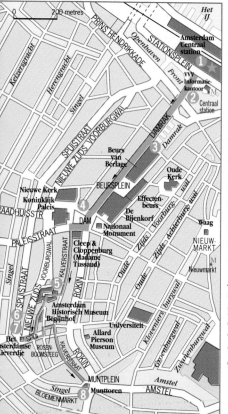

day but few stop to look at the magnificent sculptures depicting trade and industry. In its time the station was so admired that the Japanese built Tokyo station in the same style. The tower on the right displays a clock; its partner on the left has a wind-direction indicator. *With your back to the station look over to the left.*

2 VVV INFORMATIEKANTOOR (TOURIST INFORMATION)

The city's main tourist information centre is a useful reference point. It is located on the upper floor of a pretty timber building; below is the Noord-Zuid Hollandsch Koffiehaus (Coffee House), a popular spot for cakes and coffee. *Walk across Stationsplein and up Damrak.*

3 DAMRAK

On the left, little more than a duck pond, is all that remains of Amsterdam's original harbour, cut off from the sea when the station was built. Further up, the Beurs van Berlage stands on the site of the original Amsterdam Exchange. It was rebuilt in late 19th-century style in 1896 by H P Berlage and recently converted for use as a cultural centre. Next comes De Bijenkorf (The Beehive), the city's biggest department store. *Continue up Damrak to Dam square.*

4 DAM SQUARE

To the right of the city's main square is the former Stadhuis (Town Hall), completed in 1655, and renamed the Koninklijk Paleis (Royal Palace) when Louis Napoleon took up residence in 1806. It is partnered by the tall Gothic Nieuwe Kerk (New Church), begun around 1380. To the left is the National Monument commemorating the dead of World War II. The 22m obelisk contains urns of earth from each Dutch province and from Indonesia. Naked chained figures represent war victims and the inscription reads 'Never again'.
Cross the square to the right of the Peek & Cloppenburg department store and enter Kalverstraat, the city's main shopping street, all brash neon and blaring music. Halfway down, beyond Marks & Spencer, look for a lopsided gateway dated 1581.

5 AMSTERDAM HISTORISCH MUSEUM

The gate, with its figures of uniformed children, leads to the former municipal orphanage, now the Historical Museum. Walk into the arcaded courtyard and left, through glass doors, into the Civic Guard Gallery; this corridor is lined with 17th-century portraits of the city's militia units.
At the opposite end of the gallery, exit through the doors, turn right and, keeping to the left, descend two steps into the Begijnhof.

6 BEGIJNHOF

This peaceful former convent is now a home for *ongehuwde dames* (unmarried ladies). Follow the path round to the Engelsekerk (English Church), built in 1607. Opposite is Het Houten Huys (The Wooden House), built in 1460 and the oldest surviving building in Amsterdam.
Alongside is a passage leading out onto Spui. Turn right and cross to the paved area in front of the Athenaeum Bookshop.

7 HET AMSTERDAMSE LIEVERDJE

The name of this bronze statue means 'The Lovable Rascal of Amsterdam' and it is surrounded by bookshops and popular pavement cafés.
Retrace your steps past the Begijnhof entrance and walk down Rozenboomsteeg, past the elegant Empire-style building that houses Esprit. Turn right in Kalverstraat and continue all the way to the Munttoren.

8 MUNTTOREN

This grey stone tower was once a gate in the medieval city wall. The carillon of bells plays every 15 minutes. The tower was briefly used in 1672–3 for minting coins, hence its name. The walk ends just across the bridge to the right of the tower – at the Bloemenmarkt, where traders sell flowers and plants from floating barges.
To return to Dam square, simply retrace your steps down Kalverstraat.

Art is a part of daily life

The Old Side

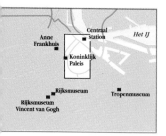

This walk covers the oldest part of the city, the Oude Zijd (Old Side) district, often simply abbreviated to OZ. The area is also known to locals as Wallen (Walls), because the two main canals – OZ Voorburgwal and OZ Achterburgwal – once lay on either side of the medieval ramparts. *Allow 2 hours*

Start on Dam square and walk across to the Grand Hotel Krasnapolsky, turning left down Warmoesstraat.

1 WARMOESSTRAAT

Number 141 is the Condomerie Het Gulden Vlies (Golden Fleece) selling nothing but giftwrapped condoms. Next door is an art gallery selling work by the squatters who live above – legally now, renting from the city council. Opposite is the Effectenbeurs, the modern Stock Exchange, housed in a building of 1913 decorated with art deco tiles and patterned brickwork. Further down is the elegant Thee en Koffiehandel, an old-fashioned tea and coffee merchant. *Opposite this shop, turn right down Wijde Kerksteeg heading for the soaring tower of Oude Kerk.*

2 OUDE KERK

This lovely church is encrusted with chapels and little houses tucked up against the walls. Ironically, too, it is hemmed in by sex cinemas and the windows of prostitutes who operate within feet of this ancient place of worship, the city's oldest surviving monument. Oude Kerk (Old Church) was founded in the 13th century; it contains 16th-century vault paintings and fine stained glass as well as the grave of Rembrandt's wife, Saskia. *Return to Warmoesstraat, turn right and take the next street left.*

3 OUDEBRUGSTEED

It is worth walking a short way down this alley to see the front of the Beurs van Berlage, and the Grasshopper Coffee Shop opposite. The latter bears an appropriate inscription given its proximity to the former Amsterdam Exchange; the legend round the roof means *nothing ventured, nothing gained*.

Return to Warmoesstraat, turning left, and continue until the street ends. Look left for a good view of the station, then turn right in Zeedijk.

4 ZEEDIJK

The first house on the left, no 1, dates from 1550 and is one of only two medieval timber-framed houses left in Amsterdam (the other is in the Begijnhof). Opposite, the frieze above the doorway of St Olafskapel is carved with skeletons. At the first bridge, Oudezijds Kolk, the ancient lock still has its original gates and machinery.

Backtrack a short way from the bridge and turn left down Sint Olafstorg, bearing left onto OZ Voorburgwal.

5 OUDE ZIJDS VOORBURGWAL

Immediately on the left several 17th-century plaques, showing Noah's Ark and shipwrights' tools, have been reset in the wall. At the first bridge look right to no 14, De Leeuwenburgh, a fine example of a step-gabled house dating from 1605. A short way further down on the right is no 40, the Museum Amstelkring. The attics of this and the two adjoining houses contain a *schuilkerken*, a clandestine Catholic church, dating from the 17th century. At the next bridge look back for a good view of St Nicolaaskerk with its neo-baroque central dome. This harbour-side church

was built in 1887, shortly after the ban on Catholic worship in the city was lifted.

If you do not want to enter the red light district, carry on up OZ Voorburgwal, past the Oude Kerk, to Damstraat, where you can turn right to return to Dam square. Otherwise, continue over the bridge and on through Korte Niezel, then turn right on OZ Achterburgwal.

6 OZ ACHTERBURGWAL

This street is lined with sex shops and red-light windows, but looking upwards you will also see some of the city's most varied canal-side architecture. Many would like to see the area cleaned up – these charming buildings would make highly desirable apartments. As it is, property owners can make so much money by renting ground floor rooms to prostitutes that they can afford to leave the rooms above unoccupied. For visitors with exotic tastes who want to sample the area after dark, no 106–108, the Theatre Casa Rosso, is one of the more 'respectable' nightclubs in the area.

Turn right into Oude Doelenstraat and you will see the Koninklijk Paleis in Dam square straight ahead. Alternatively, you can continue exploring the area by going on to the next walk.

A pause to enjoy café society

The Red Light District

Will I be safe? Will I be shocked? These two questions worry anyone who thinks of entering Amsterdam's infamous red light district. The answer to both is a qualified yes. Take precautions against theft and do not take photographs – there are plenty of gangland types about who want to remain anonymous and your camera represents a threat. The shocks come more from the explicit contents of sex shop windows than from the prostitutes themselves – their ample shapes are usually well covered by frilly lingerie or leather bondage gear.

Despite the risks, the red light district remains an essential part of the Amsterdam experience, as the large number of tour groups walking the area testify. Like every port city, commercialised sex has been available for centuries. Prostitutes with colourful names – Carmen, Blonde Venus and Joode Jet – operated here in the 17th century and paid rent to the city bailiff. He therefore had a vested interest in ensuring that they did not stray from the designated brothel area; if they did, he sent his drum and flute-playing guard to play outside the house in which they were ensconced until the combination of noise and exposure

drove them back.

Today's red light district is a pragmatic solution to a problem that will never go away. Under Dutch law, soliciting is illegal but what prostitutes and clients do in the privacy of their 'home' is regarded as their business – hence the *kamer te huur* signs (rooms to rent); officially the money that changes hands is room rent, not payment for services rendered.

The prostitutes have, in most cases, chosen this way of life for its easy money. If they change their minds, there are numerous church and government agencies willing to provide support. Drug dealing and the worst excesses of pornography are far more recent phenomena which the police and city authorities are trying to stamp out.

On the whole the red light district is colourful, it attracts tourists and contributes to the local economy, to the extent that brothel owners now sit on the Chamber of Commerce. There is a lighter side as well – the Condomerie Het Gulden Vlies (Golden Fleece) in Warmoesstraat has benefited from the post-AIDS boom in condom demand; it sells every kind imaginable – luminescent, edible or explosive, take your choice.

Not perhaps for every visitor, but Amsterdam's red light district is undeniably a tourist attraction. Amsterdam prides itself on a tolerant attitude to sexual tastes.

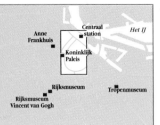

Anne Frankhuis
Centraal station
Het IJ
Koninklijk Paleis
Rijksmuseum
Tropenmuseum
Rijksmuseum Vincent van Gogh

Nieuwmarkt and the University Quarter

This walk covers some important but little-visited architectural monuments in the south of the old city. *Allow 1¹/₂ hours*

Start at Dam square and walk to the right of the Nationaal Monument, down Damstraat. Continue past the interesting shop windows of Oude Doelenstraat into Oude Hoogstraat.

1 OOST-INDISCH HUIS
A low arch beside no 24 leads into the courtyard of East India House, the former headquarters of the once-powerful trading company. The brick building dates from 1640.
Return to Oude Hoogstraat, turning right, then left onto Kloveniersburgwal.

2 TRIPPENHUIS
On the opposite bank is the palatial Trippenhuis, built between 1660 and 1664 by Justus Vingboons for the Trip brothers, who made their fortune in the armaments trade, hence the chimneys which are shaped like mortars. On this side of the canal is the Kleine (Little) Trippenhuis, also known as the House of Mr Trip's Coachman. It dates from 1696 and the frontage is only 4m wide – the modest coachman, so the story goes, said he would be happy with a house as wide as his employer's front door.
Take the next turning left, Koestraat.

3 WIJNKOPERSGILDEHUIS
Halfway down, at no 10, is the former headquarters of the wine importers' guild, a fine building dating from 1633. The

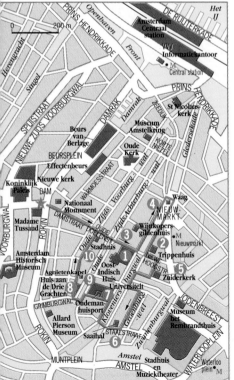

frieze above the door depicts St Urban
standing among grape vines.
Return to Kloveniersburgwal and turn left
up to Nieuwmarkt.

4 NIEUWMARKT (NEW MARKET)

This vast empty square still has a few
stalls to remind us that it was once a
major market. The dominant building is
the Waag (Weighhouse), originally built
in 1488 as a gate in the city wall. In
1617 it was fitted out with scales for
weighing naval anchors and cannon. The
octagonal tower in the centre, added in
1690, served as the Theatricum
Anatomicum, the lecture theatre of the
Surgeons' Guild (as depicted in
Rembrandt's _The Anatomy Lesson of_
Professor Deyman).
Walk down the opposite bank of
Kloveniersburgwal for a closer look at the
Trippenhuis. Note the two doors, one for
each of the Trip brothers; behind the unified
façade there were two separate residences –
the middle windows are dummies, masking
the dividing wall. Turn left in Nieuwe Hoog-
straat and first right in Zanddwarsstraat.

5 ZUIDERKERK (SOUTH CHURCH)

Straight ahead is the soaring tower of
Zuiderkerk. The church, designed in
1603 by Hendrik de Keyser, was the first
in the city to be built specifically for
Calvinist worship.
Walk to Raamgracht and, after walking
three sides of a square, continue down
Groenburgwal, turning right at the timber
lifting bridge.

6 STAALSTRAAT

This short but picturesque street is lined
with up-market antique shops. The
Saaihal (Serge Hall), no 7, was built in
1614 by Pieter de Keyser for the

clothworkers' guild.
Cross the iron lifting bridge, turn right on
Kloveniersburgwal and look for a gate on
the left just after no 82.

7 OUDEMANHUISPORT

The sculptures above the 'Gate of the
Old Men's Home' show Charity
between two ragged beggars. On the
right is the former old people's home,
built in 1786. This, and the surrounding
buildings, now form part of the
university, founded in 1876.
Walk through the passage.

8 HUIS AAN DE DRIE GRACHTEN

Facing you as you emerge is the
delightful House on the Three Canals,
built in 1609 and so called because it has
three step-gabled façades, each looking
out on to a different canal.
Walk past the house and turn right up OZ
Voorburgwal.

9 AGNIETENKAPEL

This former chapel, at no 231, was the
first home of the Atheneum Illustre, a
learned society and forerunner of the
University of Amsterdam. It now houses
exhibits from the University Historical
Collection.
Further up on the right, look for no 197, an
art deco brick gateway.

10 STADHUIS

Through the gateway to the right is The
Grand Hotel, the former Town Hall, a
classical building of 1647, built as the
Admiralty headquarters. It became the
Town Hall in 1808 when Louis
Napoleon turned the original Stadhuis,
on Dam square, into his royal palace.
Take the next turn left, Oude Doelenstraat,
to return to Dam square.

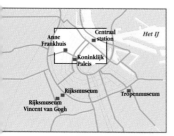

Around Brouwersgracht

This walk covers the oldest part of the canal circle, the harbour end, which was laid out from 1613. *Allow 1¹/₂ hours*

Nearby

Walking down Raadhuisstraat, take a diversion to the left a short way into Heregracht for the ornate Bartolotti House (no 170–172), and the Netherlands Theater Instituut next door (no 168).

Start at Amsterdam Centraal station. The enormous weight of this structure proved so heavy for the pile foundations that it suffered partial subsidence during construction in 1885. Walk up Damrak and take the first alley on the right, Haringpakkersteeg, then bear right in Nieuwendijk. Cross busy Martelaarsgracht, turn left up Spuistraat and take the first right, Kattengat.

1 RONDE LUTHERSE KERK

The big building on the left, with its green copper dome, is the Lutheran Round Church, built in 1668 and now used as a conference centre and concert hall. Sheltering beside the church are two attractive step-gabled houses built in 1614 by Hendrik de Keyser – De Gouden Spiegel and De Silveren Spiegel (The Golden Mirror and the Silver Mirror).
Walk on past the Round Church, into Stromarkt (Straw Market), then left on to Singel.

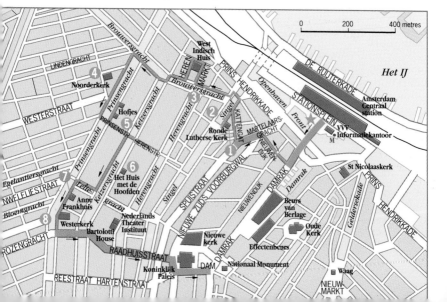

2 SINGEL

Number 7, a short way up on the left, is the smallest house in Amsterdam, only a door's width wide. The owner may have built the house like this to avoid property taxes, which were levied according to the width of the façade. To the right is Haarlemmersluis (Haarlem Lock); before the IJsselmeer was dammed and ceased to be tidal, this lock controlled the water level in the whole canal network.

Walk back up Singel, cross the bridge by the lock, turn left down the opposite bank of Singel and right into Brouwersgracht.

3 BROUWERSGRACHT

The Brewers' Canal is one of the most photogenic in the city; the right bank is lined with attractively converted 17th-century warehouses while the canal itself is crossed by numerous bridges providing a link to the three canals of the Grachtengordel. A short way up on the right, in Herenmarkt, is West-Indisch Huis, the headquarters of the West India Company from 1623.

Continue along Brouwersgracht to the Prinsengracht junction and turn left up to Noorderkerk.

4 NOORDERKERK (NORTH CHURCH)

This vast church was designed by Hendrik de Keyser and built in 1620 to serve the working-class district of Jordaan, which lies to the right. The square in front is liveliest on Saturday mornings when it hosts the *Boerenmarkt* (Farmers' Market), and on Mondays when it is the venue for a large flea market.

Cross the next bridge left and walk down the opposite bank of Prinsengracht.

5 HOFJES

Two *hofjes*, or almshouses, can be visited. Zon's Hofje (no 171 – push the door open and walk down the corridor) is a tree-shaded courtyard dating from 1765. Van Brienenhofje (nos 89–13) dates from 1804 – legend has it that Jan van Brienen, a merchant, founded it after he was rescued from imminent suffocation, having locked himself inside his own safe.

Backtrack up Prinsengracht and turn left to explore Prinsenstraat and Herenstraat, then walk up Keizersgracht.

6 HET HUIS MET DE HOOFDEN

The House with the Heads, Keizersgracht 123, was built by Hendrik de Keyser in 1623 and is decorated with busts of Greek deities – Apollo, Ceres, Ares, Athene, Dionysus and Artemis.

Turn right on Leliegracht, a cross street noted for its bookshops and especially no 44, Architectura et Natura. This specialises in books on architecture, wildlife and gardening. Turn left on Prinsengracht.

7 ANNE FRANKHUIS

Prinsengracht 263 is the house where Anne Frank wrote her famous diary while hiding with her family from the Nazis between July 1942 and August 1944. The house, with its secret annexe hidden behind a bookcase, remains exactly as it was in 1944.

Continue a short way up to Westerkerk.

8 WESTERKERK

The West Church was built to Hendrik de Keyser's design in 1623 and its tower, the tallest in Amsterdam, can be climbed for a bird's eye view of the canal circle.

From Westerkerk, turn left and follow Raadhuisstraat to return to Dam square.

Jordaan

Jordaan is the sock-shaped district which wraps round the western half of the canal circle. Despite its name (Jordaan means garden), this was the industrial quarter of 17th-century Amsterdam where noxious trades were carried on. Once a slum it is now a friendly neighbourhood of inexpensive shops and cafés, and numerous hidden almshouses *(hofjes). Allow 1¹/₂ hours*

From Dam square walk down Raadhuisstraat past Westerkerk and over the bridge to the left bank of Prinsengracht. Walk down this canal and take the second left, Bloemgracht.

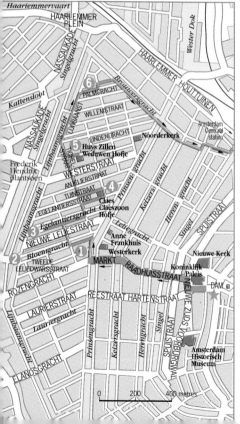

1 BLOEMGRACHT

The Flower Canal is also known as the Herengracht (Gentlemen's Canal) of the Jordaan because it has the most splendid houses. The step-gabled buildings, nos 87–91, date from 1642 and belong to an organisation dedicated to preserving the many ornate buildings in this area designed by the Golden Age architect, Hendrik de Keyser.
At the second bridge turn right into Tweede Leliedwarsstraat.

2 TWEEDE LELIEDWARSSTRAAT

Craft shops and art galleries line this short street with the formidable name which means 'Second Lily Cross Street'. All the short intersecting streets are numbered from east to west: Eerste (First), Tweede (Second) and so on, and all the main streets are named after flowers.
Cross Nieuwe Leliestraat and take the next left.

3 EGELANTIERSGRACHT

The beautifully named Eglantine

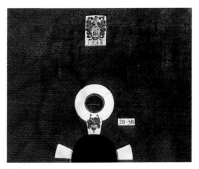

Palmgracht's unusual name-plate

(Honeysuckle) Street has a well restored almshouse, Sint Andrieshofje, at no 107, dated 1617 and one of the oldest in the city. Enter to see a remarkable Delft-tiled passageway with a hidden garden. From outside the building turn round and walk up the canal, noting the plaques of no 89, two tailors at work, and nos 61–63, a hooded hawk. Plaques like these, often relating to the householder's profession, were once used to identify houses.
At the next bridge look right for a good view of Westerkerk then turn left down Tweede Egelantiersdwarsstraat. There are scores of excellent shops along this street. Turn right in Egelantiersstraat and look for the almshouse entrance at no 52.

4 CLAES CLAESZOON HOFJE
This almshouse consists of 23 smaller houses dating from 1620 which display a fine sequence of gable styles.
Turn left in Eerste Egelantiersdwarsstraat and left again in Tuinstraat. Halfway up on the left is Regensboog-Liefdehofje, with 17th-century step gables. Take the next right, Tweede Tuindwarsstraat, cross Anjelierstraat (Carnation Street) then continue down Tichelstraat and turn right in Karthuizerstraat.

5 HUYS ZILLEN WEDUWEN HOFJE
This street is dominated by the long façade of the 1650 almshouse – the 'House of the Elderly Widows' – the biggest and best of the Jordaan *hofjes*.
Return to Tichelstraat, looking left for a last view of Westerkerk. Turn right onto Lijnbaanstraat and walk down this canal, past the iron lifting bridge on Willemstraat. Turn right in Palmgracht.

6 PALMGRACHT
Here are several more fine houses. Numbers 73–79, on the right, date from 1673 and their plaque depicts a bunch of radishes. On the left, at nos 28–38, is the Boffschehofje, founded in 1648 by Pieter Adriaenszoon Raep, whose surname means turnip, hence the vegetable depicted on the plaque.
At the end of Palmgracht turn right on to Brouwersgracht. Follow this canal, with its numerous bridges, boats and waterfowl, all the way back to the centre of Amsterdam, heading for the copper-green dome of the Round Lutheran Church (see Walk 4) visible in the distance.

HOFJES
Many of the *hofjes* in the Jordaan district were built by wealthy merchants for housing sick or retired employees and their families. The pensioners were expected to work in return for this charity and the characteristic inner courtyard was originally used as a *bleekveld*, a bleaching field, for laying out cloth to bleach in the sun. Many are now beautifully planted communal gardens.

Look up and feast your eyes on gable art. Obliged
to conform in matters architectural, decorative
gables express Amsterdam individuality

Gable Types

Amsterdam has been described as a city of 'architectural good manners', a city of few ostentatious buildings but of a myriad charming details.

Seventeenth-century planning laws ensured that all houses were built of brick or stone to standard widths, so that canal-side homeowners had limited scope for placing their personal stamp on the property. One way was to vary the number and size of windows in the façade; huge expanses of gleaming glass advertised the wealth of the owner, since glass was an expensive commodity. Another way of expressing individualism was to cover the crown and sides of the gable with sculptures or ornamental frills and flourishes.

Gables were originally very plain. They were designed to disguise the roof ridge, built at right angles to the canal, and the earliest type was the point gable, a simple inverted 'V' that precisely followed the shape of the roof timbers.

Next came the spout gable which is the same as a point gable except with a chimney-like rectangular protusion from the point; these two types are commonly seen on the earliest surviving warehouses.

By 1600 the more ornate step step gable was in use for domestic buildings and it remained in vogue until Philips Vingboons designed the first neck gable, shaped like the shoulders and neck of a wine bottle, for the Cromhouthuisen (now the Bijbels Museum) in 1638. This quickly became fashionable, and was joined by the bell gable in 1660.

From 1670 the owners of grand houses on the Golden Bend of the canal circle began to reject the traditional Dutch style. Sandstone was used for the façades instead of brick and the frontages were now too wide to be spanned by a single gable. Instead the roof line was hidden by pediments, balustrades and cornices, often embellished with baroque swags and garlands or neo-classical sculpture, in the style of Italian *palazzi*. Even so, the graciously shaped gable, the trademark of Amsterdam architecture, remained in use for humbler homes right up to the present century, and you only have to take a short stroll along the canal circle to realise just how well these simple geometric shapes lend themselves to an infinite number of variations.

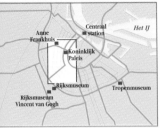

The Golden Bend

The canal circle's Golden Bend was so named because of the size and splendour of the houses and the wealth of its former inhabitants.
Allow 1¹/₂ hours

Begin on Dam square. Walk to the left of the Koninklijk Paleis (Royal Palace) and cross the busy junction to walk down Raadhuisstraat.

1 RAADHUISSTRAAT

This street was laid out in 1894, cutting a broad swathe through the canal circle. The huge building on the right, with its minaret-like towers, was the main Post Office until 1991 and is now being converted to a shopping galleria. Number 12 is the Spaarpotten (Piggy Bank) Museum. To the right, down Herengracht, is the ornate Bartolotti House, built in 1621 by Hendrik de Keyser for Guillielmo Bartolotti, a wealthy brewer

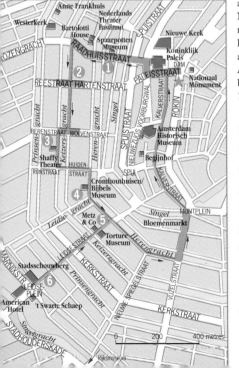

and banker. Next door is the beautiful Netherlands Theater Instituut with its neck gables, dating from 1637. On the left-hand side of Raadhuisstraat is an attractive art deco arcade, designed by A L van Gendt, the same architect who built the Concertgebouw.
Turn left to walk down Keizersgracht.

Nearby

From Leidseplein it is a short walk to the renowned Rijksmuseum where you can also join Walk 7: The Museum Quarter. Simply turn left in Leidseplein, alongside 't Swarte Schaep, down Korte Leidsedwarsstraat, a street lined with cafés and restaurants. At the end you will see Museumbrug (Museum Bridge) to your right, leading to the Rijksmuseum.

2 CROSS STREETS

As you walk, it is worthwhile exploring the short cross streets to right and left, linking the three main canals. Their names indicate that this part of the city was once the haunt of furriers: Reestraat means Roe Street, Harten means deer, Beren bears. Wolven is obviously wolves while Huidenstraat means Hide Street and Runstraat is named after the bark used in the leather tanning process. *Just after Berenstraat look for the huge building on the right inscribed 'Felix Meritus'.*

3 SHAFFY THEATER

This neo-classical building was founded in 1788 as a lecture theatre and concert hall by the Felix Meritus ('Happy through Achievement') Society, a patrician body whose aim was to promote knowledge of the arts and sciences. Haydn, Brahms and Grieg all conducted here. From 1946 it was the headquarters of the Communist Party, which was well supported immediately after World War II because of its role in the Resistance. Since 1960 the building has been used as a theatre specialising in experimental works and is named after the actor, Ramses Shaffy. *At the next bridge turn left down Huidenstraat and right down Herengracht.*

4 CROMHOUTHUISEN/BIJBELS MUSEUM

Numbers 364 to 370 on the right, derive their name from Jacob Cromhout, a builder whose trademark (depicted on a plaque to the right of the door to no 366) was a crooked stick – the literal meaning of his surname. Today this fine group of houses, dating from 1662, houses the Biblical Museum. *Continue down Herengracht and stop to*

look at the succession of bridges marking the junction with Leidsegracht. Continue and take the first right, Leidsestraat.

5 LEIDSESTRAAT

A short way up on the right is Metz & Co, a department store founded in 1740 but, despite its age, now selling ultra-chic modern furnishings. At no 27 the Torture Museum is much loved by children for its grisly displays of genuine antique guillotines and similar nasty implements. *Carry on up Leidsestraat to Leidseplein.*

6 LEIDSEPLEIN

This is the centre of Amsterdam nightlife where you will find a mixture of up-market establishments and cheap fast-food outlets which have earned the square its nickname, 'La Place de la Mayonnaise'. On the right is the Stadsschouwburg (City Theatre), a venerable institution founded in 1894. Alongside is the eccentric art deco American Hotel, built in 1904 to the design of Willem Kromhout. A visit to the Café Americain inside is a must for its elegant stained glass, murals and Tiffany-style chandeliers. On the left-hand side of the square is 't Swarte Schaep (The Black Sheep) a restaurant dated 1627 and renowned for its Dutch-French cuisine. In the side streets to the right and left are the city's two big rock music venues, Paradiso and Melkweg. *To return to Dam square, backtrack down Leidsestraat and turn right down Herengracht where the most splendid of all the houses on the Golden Bend are located, most of them now embassy and bank premises. Turn left in Vijzelstraat to reach Muntplein and then follow Kalverstraat all the way back to Dam square.*

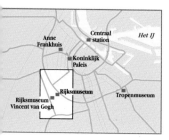

The Museum Quarter

This walk combines Amsterdam's three major museums with the best of the city's up-market shopping. *Allow 1½ hours*

Start at the Rijksmuseum. This is served by trams 6, 7 and 10 but a more enjoyable way to reach it is by Museumboat (departures every 30 minutes from 10am to 3.15pm daily from in front of Amsterdam Centraal station).

1 RIJKSMUSEUM

This palatial building was designed by P J H Cuypers in 1885 and bears a strong resemblance to his other great work, Amsterdam Centraal station. Intended as a 'cathedral of the arts' it was built in neo-gothic style and embellished with

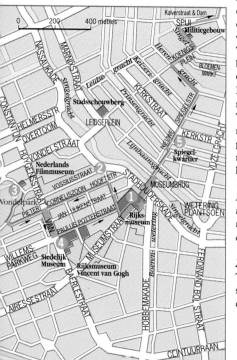

sculptures, murals and tilework depicting various kinds of artistic endeavour. The vast collection inside was begun in the 18th century by William V of Orange and given impetus by Louis Napoleon who set up the Grand Musée Royal in the Koninklijk Paleis in a bid to make Amsterdam a major European centre for the arts. Today the collection consists of 7 million works of art, including 5,000 paintings. There are more than 250 rooms in the museum of which less than half are open to the public.

Walk under the echoing tunnel beneath the Rijksmuseum, the haunt of buskers, street traders and hot dog vendors, and turn right. Cross Jan Luijkenstraat and turn left onto Pieter Corneliszoon Hooftstraat.

2 P C HOOFTSTRAAT

This is Amsterdam's most elegant shopping street, the place where Dutch celebrities and the wealthy élite come to buy Italian designer-label fashions, works of art, furnishings or just a box of handmade chocolates. Window shopping here is a pleasure and there are several elegant 'designer' cafés.

After crossing Van Baerlestraat, continue up P C Hooftstraat to enter Vondelpark.

3 VONDELPARK

This green oasis in the centre of the city was laid out in 1865 in the 'English' landscape style and named after the 17th-century Dutch poet, Joost van den Vondel, popularly known as the 'Shakespeare of The Netherlands'. The days when the park was one vast hippy encampment have gone but there are outdoor concerts – everything from classics to punk rock – throughout the summer. The Nederlands Filmmuseum, to the right of the entrance, shows a wide selection of 'art' and historic films, and there is an exhibition on the history of cinema.

Retrace your steps down P C Hooftstraat and turn right in Van Baerlestraat. Take the second left, Paulus Potterstraat, for the other two big museums.

4 THE STEDELIJK MUSEUM AND RIJKSMUSEUM VINCENT VAN GOGH

The Stedelijk Museum houses the city's collection of modern art, though you would not guess so from the turreted red-brick building itself, built in neo-Renaissance style in 1895. By contrast the Rijksmuseum Vincent Van Gogh is stark and ultra-modern. It was designed by Gerrit Rietveld and completed in 1973. Van Gogh's vibrant paintings inside are a great deal more colourful than the building.

Continue down Paulus Potterstraat past Coster Diamonds (whose workshops can be

visited). Turn right, then left, passing through the Rijksmuseum tunnel. Cross busy Stadhouderskade to reach Museumbrug (Museum Bridge) and head straight on for the Spiegelkwartier.

5 THE SPIEGELKWARTIER

This area can be considered an extension of the Museum Quarter but with a difference: the works of art on show here are all for sale. Many antique and fine art dealers set up shop here shortly after the Rijksmuseum opened in 1885 to capture the trade of visiting art lovers. Every shop along Spiegelgracht, Nieuwe Spiegelstraat and Kerkstraat (the side street to the right) is full of treasures and you can browse for hours.

Continue to the end of Nieuwe Spiegelstraat, past the Institute for Contemporary Art (temporary exhibitions, open Monday to Friday 11am to 5pm, Saturday 11am to 9pm), then turn left on Herengracht, with its palatial bank and embassy premises. Take the first right, Koenigsplein, which passes the floating flower market, the Bloemenmarkt, on the right. Bear left along Singel to see no 423, the Militiegebouw (Militia Building), built in 1606 as the city arsenal. Take the next right, Spui, and the next left, Kalverstraat, to return to Dam square.

An eye on the future in Vondelpark

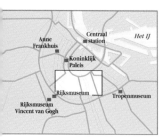

Around the Amstel

Amsterdam is named after the River Amstel which once flowed through the heart of the city. The original course has since been filled in but on this walk visitors will see the stretch that survives, a broad rolling watercourse that brings the canal circle to an abrupt end in the east of the city.
Allow 1 hour

Nearby

Kerkstraat runs parallel to Keizersgracht to the left. On the Kerkstraat/ Reguliersgracht junction there is an unusual church built in 1670 in timber as a temporary measure – a bigger brick church was planned but never built.

Start at Muntplein. Its landmark tower, the Munttoren, was given its elegant steeple by Hendrik de Keyser in 1619. Cross the chaotic junction and walk down Reguliersbreestraat to the cinema halfway down on the left.

1 TUSCHINSKI CINEMA

This wonderful art deco cinema stands incongruously surrounded by fast-food outlets and tacky souvenir shops. Founded by Abram Tuschinski, a Polish Jew who died at Auschwitz, it opened in 1921 and retains all its original fittings – go inside to admire the lavish carpets, murals and lamps of the foyer and to check what films are showing.
Turn right out of the cinema for Rembrandtplein.

2 REMBRANDTPLEIN

A statue of Rembrandt, on the right, looks down with a bemused expression on the square that bears his name. The

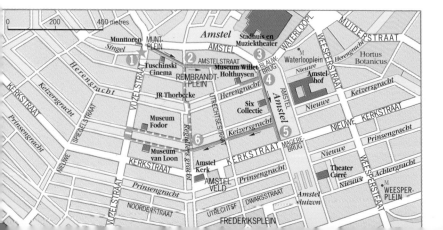

square is completely surrounded by pavement cafés, commercialised but nevertheless a lively spot at night.
Walk down Amstelstraat, passing the formal gardens of the Willet-Holthuysen Museum on the right, to the Amstel.

3 AMSTEL

Straight ahead is the unmissable bulk of the Stadhuis/Muziektheater complex, considered by locals to be a blot on the landscape and completed in 1988. Alongside is the Blauwbrug of a century earlier, modelled on the flamboyant Pont Alexandre III in Paris. This is a more restrained version with boat-shaped piers and lampstands topped by the imperial crown of Amsterdam's coat of arms. On the opposite bank, to the right, you will see the long façade of the Amstelhof, built in 1683 and still in use for its original purpose as a home for the elderly.
Turn right and follow the Amstel embankment to the first bridge.

4 HERENGRACHT

Look right from the bridge down this leafy canal with its patrician houses. If you have the time walk down the right-hand embankment to visit the Willet-Holthuysen Museum, no 605, and see its authentic and stately 18th-century interiors.
Continue along the Amstel, past no 218 which houses the Six Collectie, heading for the white lifting bridge spanning the river.

5 MAGEREBRUG

The 'Skinny Bridge' is over 300 years old and derives its name from an earlier, even narrower, bridge across the Amstel. This has become one of the cherished landmarks of Amsterdam and, if you wait a while, you may see a huge barge

carefully negotiate a passage underneath. On the opposite bank is the bulky Theater Carré, built in 1887 as a circus venue, now used to stage popular musical productions.
Retrace your steps to Keizersgracht and walk down the left-hand embankment, noting the variety of gable styles represented on the buildings opposite. Cross Utrechtsestraat and continue along Keizersgracht, looking out for the huge figure of Neptune on the gable of no 695.

6 REGULIERSGRACHT

The next crossing marks the junction of Keizersgracht and Reguliersgracht, photogenic spot featured on countless postcards. There are five bridges spanning the junction and long vistas open up in every direction, each embankment lined by tipsy leaning houses.

Walkers now have a choice. Continue along the north side of Keizersgracht and you will come to the Museum Fodor (no 609) on the right, with its displays of modern art, and the palatial Museum Van Loon (no 672) opposite. Alternatively turn right, down Reguliersgracht, to return to Rembrandtplein.

Reguliersgracht: Amsterdam at its prettiest

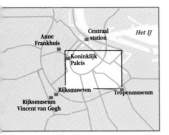

Jodenbuurt

Amsterdam's Jewish Quarter has been redeveloped since World War II but it contains several notable monuments, including Rembrandt's house. *Allow 1 hour*

Take the Metro from Amsterdam Centraal station and alight at the first stop, Nieuwmarkt.

Nearby

Just beyond the Portugese Synagogue, on Nieuwe Herengracht, there is the entrance to Hortus Botanicus, the Botanical Garden. Beyond, in the leafy suburb of Plantage, visitors will find Amsterdam's zoo, Artis Magistra.

1 NIEUWMARKT METRO

Protestors battled with police on 'Blue Monday', 24 March 1975, in an attempt to stop houses in the Nieuwmarkt area from being demolished to build the Metro. Murals and a giant demolition ball in the station recall that event.
Take the exit marked Nieuwmarkt/Sint Antoniesbreestraat and turn left down the latter street.

2 DE PINTO HUIS

Number 69 Sint Antoniesbreestraat is an Italianate house dating from 1605 and now a public library. Go in to see the painted panels and ornate ceiling (open Monday and Wednesday 2pm to 8pm, Friday 2pm to 5pm, Saturday 11am to 2pm). The house was built for Isaac de Pinto, a Jewish refugee from Portugal who became a wealthy banker. This building was saved from demolition by the force of public protest in the 1970s when the rest of the street was redeveloped. Through the gate opposite there is a good view of

the Zuiderkerk.

Just beyond this house, on the left, is a lock called Sint Antoniessluis. Look left for a good view of the Montelbaanstoren, built in 1512 as part of the city's defences, and of the warehouses lining Oude Schans. Turn round and you will see Rembrandt's house.

3 MUSEUM HET REMBRANDTHUIS

This lovely house was built in 1606 (the year of Rembrandt's birth) and cost the artist 13,000 guilders when he bought it in 1639, a considerable amount of money. Perhaps that is why Rembrandt once ended up in court for cheating – having ordered some wood to repair his house, Rembrandt fraudulently charged the cost to his neighbour, the banker Isaac de Pinto. The banker sued but the judge ruled that, as de Pinto's name was on the bill, he must pay!

Turn right beside the Rembrandthuis and left onto Waterlooplein. Every day except Sunday, visitors will find a flea market in full swing, a remnant of the old market where Jewish traders set up their stalls. Walk through the market to the huge church on the left.

4 MOZES EN AÄRONKERK.

This vast neo-classical church dates from 1841 and many houses were demolished to make way for its construction, including the birthplace of Baruch Spinoza (1632–77), the Jewish-born philosopher.

Cross busy Mr Visserplein (named after L E Visser, the Jewish former head of the Dutch Supreme Court) to the massive brick synagogue on the left.

5 PORTUGESE SYNAGOGUE

When it was completed in 1675 this Sephardic synagogue was the biggest in

the world. The untouched interior can be visited. In the square alongside, Marie Andriessen's *Dokwerker* statue commemorates the general strike of 1941 led by dockers and transport workers in protest against Jewish persecution.

Cross Jonas Daniel Meijerplein (named after a remarkable lawyer who, in 1796 and aged only 16, became the first Jew to be admitted to the Dutch bar) to the synagogue complex opposite.

6 JOODS HISTORISCH MUSEUM

The four buildings of the former Ashkenazic synagogue complex date from the mid-17th century and now make up the Jewish Historical Museum. Walk through the connecting glass corridor for a glimpse of the museum and, perhaps, to sample kosher cakes in the museum café.

Leave by the main entrance, walk down Turfsteeg and cross Waterlooplein to the Stadhuis, aiming for the glass-covered arcade straight ahead.

7 NORMAAL AMSTERDAMS PEIL

The arcade contains various exhibits illustrating the standard ordnance datum adopted by Dutch surveyors in 1648 (explanatory leaflets are available in several languages).

Continue through the arcade and turn left past the Muziektheater box office and Café Vienna. Leave the building by the doors straight ahead; look left for a view of Blauwbrug and right, down the Amstel, to Munttoren. Turn right for the black marble memorial slab to the Jews who died in World War II, then follow Zwanenburgwal, alongside the Stadhuis, back to the Rembrandthuis; the Metro entrance alongside will take you back to Amsterdam Centraal station.

The Docklands

Discover the remains of maritime Amsterdam in an area of the city which visitors rarely penetrate. *Allow 2 hours*

Start from Amsterdam Centraal station and walk left, past the VVV Informatiekantoor (tourist information centre), along Oosterdokskade. Use the pedestrian crossing to reach the other side of Prins Hendrikkade and turn right.

1 SCHREIERSTOREN

You will soon reach the 'Tower of Tears', built in 1480 as part of the city wall. By tradition sailors' wives watched their husbands' ships depart from this point. There are several plaques: one depicts a weeping woman, another reads 'Eerste Schipvaart Naar Ostindie 1595' (First Voyage to the East Indies, 1595) and a third records that Henry Hudson's ship, the *Half Moon*, set out from here in 1609 on a voyage that led to the discovery of the Hudson River and Manhattan Island. *Look right for a good view of Zuiderkerk, then continue round Prins Hendrikkade.*

2 SCHEEPVAARTHUIS

The next building on the right is 'Maritime House', a richly decorated art deco building and the best example of Amsterdam School architecture in the city. It was built by J M

van der Mey in 1916 and is covered in fanciful brick sculptures.

At the far end of the building turn right down Buiten Bantammerstraat and cross the art deco bridge with its seahorse motifs. Turn left down Oude Waal and head for the tower at the end.

3 MONTELBAANSTOREN

This tower was built in 1512 when the city's defences were extended to run up the side of the Oude Schans (literally 'Old Bulwark') basin. The openwork spire was added in 1606 by Hendrik de Keyser.

Turn left up Kalkmarkt, noting no 8 with its steamship plaque, right on Prins Hendrikkade and right down 's Gravenhekje, noting the West India Company warehouse to the left, dated 1642. Turn left down Rapenburg. An ugly, but unavoidable, stretch lies ahead, caused by the entrance to the IJ tunnel, which links the city to the northern harbour. Turn right, cross the tunnel sliproad by the pedestrian lights, walk to the right of the fire station down Anne Frankstraat, then left down Nieuwe Herengracht. Walk past the lock on Rapenburgerplein, turn right across the next bridge and right through a monumental arch inscribed Entrepôtdok.

4 ENTREPÔTDOK

This vast complex consists of 84 warehouses, dating from the 19th century, which have been converted to apartments, named in alphabetical order after Dutch cities.

At the end, turn left, climb the steps and cross the bridge to the right for a view of the Kromhout Museum. Go back over the bridge, walking down Hoogte Kadijk, and take the first right, Overhaalsgang. Cross the footbridge, looking right for a view of the 1814 De Gooyer windmill.

5 OOSTERKERK

On the opposite side of the road from the footbridge is the Oosterkerk, built in 1670 to serve the local shipbuilding community. The church stands on a man-made island, Wittenburg, with another to the right (Oostenburg) and a third to the left (Kattenburg). The islands date from 1650 and were constructed to provide dockyards where the warships of the Dutch navy were built.

Turn left in front of the church and walk down to the former Zeemagazijn.

6 NEDERLANDS SCHEEPVAART MUSEUM

The Zeemagazijn, or Admiralty arsenal, was built in 1656 and now houses the outstanding Scheepvaart (Maritime) Museum. This is well worth a visit, especially to explore the East Indiaman moored in the dock alongside, to experience something of life aboard a typical 17th-century cargo ship.

To return to Amsterdam Centraal station, catch bus 22 or 28 from Kattenburgergracht. The alternative is a rather dreary walk along traffic-choked Prins Hendrikkade.

The Tower of Tears witnessed many sad farewells

What to See

AGNIETENKAPEL

The Agnietenkapel is a simple but graceful chapel dating from 1470 and once part of the convent of St Agnes. In 1632 it was taken over by the Atheneum Illustre, a learned body out of which the University of Amsterdam was later to evolve. Part of the chapel was converted into a lecture theatre, the Grote Gehoorzal, which has a fine wooden ceiling decorated with Renaissance motifs and a portrait of Minerva, goddess of wisdom. The walls of the theatre are hung with 17th-century portraits of illustrious and learned figures of the age. The rest of the building houses the Universiteitsmuseum (University Museum) a collection covering the history of education and student life in the city.

Oudezijds Voorburgwal 231 (tel: 525 3339).

The fascinating Amstelkring Museum

Open: Monday to Friday 9am–5pm
Admission charge
Trams 4, 9, 16, 24, or 25
Nearby: Allard Pierson Museum, University Quarter (see **Walk 3**).

ALLARD PIERSON MUSEUM

This little visited museum houses the University of Amsterdam's rich collection of archaeological material - mainly from ancient Egypt, Rome, Tuscany and the Near East. The museum also displays plaster casts of ancient Greek and Roman sculpture and occasionally mounts excellent special exhibitions on specific themes.

Oude Turfmarkt 127 (tel: 525 2556)
Open: Tuesday to Friday 10am–5pm, Saturday, Sunday and public holidays 1pm–5pm
Admission charge
Trams 4, 9, 16, 24, or 25
Nearby: Agnietenkapel, the University Quarter (see **Walk 3**).

Bicycles are part of the Amsterdam landscape

AMSTELKRING, MUSEUM

The Amstelkring Museum is also known as *Ons Lieve Heer op Solder* (Our Lord in the Attic) because concealed in the roof space of this group of three houses, there is a clandestine Catholic church. The delightful museum thus provides two quite different experiences. Downstairs is a fine example of a wealthy merchant's residence, built by Jan Hartman in 1661, complete with contemporary furnishings. One sober-looking cupboard opens up to reveal bawdy, low-life scenes painted on the insides of the door. Upstairs, by contrast, is a splendid baroque church with ingenious foldaway pulpit and altar, and hiding places for the priest and communion plate.

Clandestine churches such as this date from the *Alteratie*, the Alteration of 1578. Until then Amsterdam was a Catholic city, but tolerant of Protestants and freethinkers, refugees from persecution in other parts of Europe. Calvinists formed a large and influential group, but they were forbidden from holding public services until they rioted in 1566, breaking into the city's churches and smashing statues, an event known as the *Beeldenstorm*, the Iconoclasm.

Order was restored when Calvinists were given their own church in the city, but this in turn provoked a reaction from Philip II of Spain, Holy Roman Emperor and staunch defender of the Catholic faith. He sent 10,000 troops under the Duke of Alva, Fernando Alvarez de Toledo, to restore strict Catholic order in The Netherlands. Many Calvinists in Amsterdam were executed and others fled to England.

The Dutch revolt against Spanish repression began in 1572 under the leadership of William the Silent, Prince of Orange, whose volunteer army slowly drove the Spanish southwards, to the area of modern Belgium. They liberated Amsterdam in 1578, the year of the *Alteratie*, so called because Protestants then took over all the city's institutions and Catholicism, from then onwards, was banned – hence the growth of secret churches, of which the Amstelkring Museum has the best-preserved example.

In 1661, when this church was built, Catholics still went to great lengths to conceal their worship. By 1740, when the church was remodelled and given its galleries, capable of seating 150 people, it could scarcely still be operating without the knowledge of the authorities, who must simply have turned a blind eye. The ban on Catholicism was finally lifted in the 19th century when the nearby church of Sint Nicolaas was built, now standing forlorn and rarely used on the harbour, opposite Amsterdam Centraal station.

Oudezijds Voorburgwal 40
(tel: 624 6604)
Open: Monday to Saturday 10am–5pm,
Sunday and public holidays 1pm–5pm
(closed 1 January)
Admission charge
Trams 4, 9, 16, 24, or 25
*Nearby: Oude Kerk (see **Churches**).*

Amsterdam Historisch Museum

The Amsterdam Historical Museum is a must for those who want to understand the history and development of the city. It is located just off Kalverstraat, the city's main shopping thoroughfare. The entrance is easy to miss amidst all the brash neon – just a narrow leaning gateway decorated with the imperial crown and triple cross of Amsterdam's coat of arms. Below, a sculptural relief of

The Golden Age relived in the Historical Museum

children dressed in blue and red uniforms reminds us that the museum occupies the buildings of the former municipal orphanage, founded in 1580 on the site of St Lucy's convent. When you pass through the arch, the museum café is on the right, occupying the former convent dairy. It serves excellent pancakes and is known as 'Old Goliath' after the huge wooden fairground figures of David and Goliath standing at one end.

Beyond lies a series of beautifully restored buildings designed by two leading 17th-century architects, Hendrik de Keyser and Jacob van Campen. They surround quiet cobbled courtyards where the orphanage children used to play. The prestige of the buildings is an indication of the city's enlightened policy in providing for the care of the poor – long before the idea of a welfare state was conceived.

The museum itself begins with an illuminated map of the city and a population growth column; both are divided into 25-year periods which light up in sequence to show how the city and its population have grown from a tiny 13th-century fishing community to the huge city of today. Other maps show the position of the original dam across the Amstel and its associated sea dyke walls. Best of all is the woodcut of 1544 by Cornelis Anthoniszoon, a three-dimensional bird's-eye view of the city and its bustling harbour.

The next two rooms contain archaeological finds, reconstructed rooms and contemporary paintings to illustrate life and industry in the medieval city. Another room is devoted to the Miracle of Amsterdam which occurred in 1345. The rather unsavoury details concern a dying man who was given communion as part of the Last Rites but who vomited up the host; this was thrown on a fire but found intact in the embers the next day. A miracle was declared and Amsterdam became a pilgrimage centre, so important that even the Holy Roman Emperor, Maximilian I, came to be cured of an illness. The Miracle is still celebrated today by up to 10,000 Catholics who take part in the *Stille Omgang* – the Silent Procession – which passes through the city's streets every 17 March.

Rooms 5 to 8 illustrate aspects of the city in the Golden Age (17th century). Another illuminated map shows the main Dutch voyages of discovery that set out from Amsterdam from 1595 looking first for a northeastern passage to the East Indies, then blazing a trail around the Cape of Good Hope. Typical eastern imports are displayed – blue and white Chinese porcelain that gave rise to the Dutch Delftware industry, sugar, tea and spices. A colourful contemporary painting shows Dam square at that time, crowded with beggars, street musicians, artists selling their products, prosperous burghers in their finery – in fact little different from today, except for the changes in dress!

The rooms beyond look at the art and crafts of the 17th century and a small loft above Room 10 is devoted to carillon music, a distinctive feature of the city's churches; here you can sit at a keyboard and play tunes on the bells suspended above.

To reach Room 11 cross the Civic Guard Gallery, a glassed-in public thoroughfare hung with militia company portraits. Room 11 itself contains more group portraits – of the regents who supervised the city's charitable institutions – and some big pictures of happy orphanage life, a far cry from the experiences of Dickens' Oliver Twist.

The museum tour concludes with a look at bourgeois life in 18th-century Amsterdam, all ponderous furniture and silverware, before livening up again with a brief account of industry. Look out, too, for stimulating temporary exhibitions, covering anything from the history of gay rights in the city to historic prints and postcards.

Entrances at Kalverstraat 92 and Sint Luciensteeg 27 (tel: 523 1822)
Open: daily 11am–5pm (closed 1 Jan)
Admission charge
Trams 1, 2, 4, 5, 9, 16, 24 or 25
Nearby: Begijnhof.

Arms and armour on display in the Historical Museum testify to the vital importance of military might in the turbulent history of The Netherlands

Anne Frankhuis

The Anne Frank House attracts more then half a million visitors a year and in summer it is essential to go early in the day to avoid long queues and crowded rooms. The house is tucked away on quiet Prinsengracht in the shadow of Westerkerk's tower, whose bells are lyrically described in Anne Frank's famous diary. It is a typical merchant's house, built in 1635, with an *achterhuis,* or back extension, added in 1740. In this attic the Frank family hid from July 1942 to August 1944.

The Franks had already escaped from Nazi persecution once in their lives; in 1933 they left their native Frankfurt, where Anne was born in 1929, and moved to Amsterdam, where they lived happily enough for seven years.

On 14 May 1940, the Nazis bombed Rotterdam: 800 people, mostly innocent civilians, were killed, 24,000 homes were destroyed and 50,000 people were left homeless. The Germans warned that they would next bomb Den Haag (The

Hague), then Utrecht and all other Dutch cities in turn. Faced with such appalling aggression the Dutch had no choice but to surrender on 15 May: that night, knowing what was to come, 150 Jews in Amsterdam committed suicide.

Anti-Jewish measures began in earnest in 1940 with a series of prohibitive proclamations: Jews could not enter public places – swimming pools, parks and cinemas – or use public transport; all Jewish businesses had to be registered. In February 1941 the Jewish Quarter of the city was closed off and the first of a series of round-ups, *razzias,* began. Thousands were arrested, herded into trains and sent off to Westerbork, a concentration camp on the Dutch/German border.

In 1942, Anne Frank's father, Otto, decided that the best course of action was to 'dive' – *onderduiken* – simply to disappear. He prepared a hiding

Inside the haunting Anne Frank House

place in the house that served as his company's office and warehouse. On 5 July a deportation order arrived, calling up Otto's eldest daughter, Margot, for 'work' at Westerbork. The next morning the family disappeared into the attic of Prinsengracht 263, their hiding place protected by nothing more solid than a bookcase concealing the stairs to the back of the house.

The Franks were joined by the van Daan family and a dentist, Albert Dussell. For two years this clandestine household survived with the help of Otto Frank's Dutch partners and his two office girls, Miep and Elli. Food was provided by a local greengrocer, one of several who played their part in the Resistance by supplying 'divers'.

Not everyone was so altruistic. Someone – never identified – betrayed the Franks to the Nazis in 1944. They were arrested and sent to Westerbork, now a staging post for Bergen-Belsen, where Anne Frank died of hunger and disease in March 1945, aged 15. Of all the eight members of the secret household, only Otto Frank survived.

The Anne Frank House remains as it was in 1944, bare of furniture, which was looted after the family was deported. There are magazine pictures of film stars pasted on the wall by Anne and pencil marks recording the heights of the two growing sisters. The front of the building is used for exhibitions mounted by the Anne Frank Foundation, which is dedicated to combating prejudice, racism and discrimination in all its forms.

Anne Frank's diary, *Het Achterhuis*, was found lying on the floor after the family was arrested. It has since been published in 51 languages and vividly records the daily routine of life in the

The house where the Frank family hid for two years

secret annexe, as well as the growing maturity of a naturally gifted writer, doomed to a tragic end. One of the last entries in the diary states; 'I want to live on after my death'. That wish, at least, has been achieved.

Prinsengracht 263 (tel: 626 4533)
Open: June to August, Monday to Saturday 9am–7pm; Sunday and public holidays 10am – 7pm. September to May, Monday to Saturday 9am – 5pm; Sunday and public holidays 10am–5pm (closed 25 December, 1 January and Yom Kippur)
Admission charge
Trams 13 or 17
*Nearby: Westerkerk (see **Churches**).*

BEGIJNHOF

The Begijnhof is a secluded oasis of peace in the bustling heart of the city. The entrance, easily missed, is a narrow door on Spui that leads into a flowery tree-shaded courtyard where neat gardens front some of Amsterdam's most charming houses. Number 34, known as the Het Houten Huis or Wooden House, is the oldest surviving in the city, dating back to around 1470.

The Begijnhof was founded in 1346 as a convent for Beguines, named after

The tranquil calm of the Begijnhof

Lambert de Begué who founded the order in Liège in the 12th century. The order – popular in the Low Countries and Germany – enabled women to live in a convent, devoting themselves to charitable work, but without taking vows of poverty, obedience and chastity. They remained free to own property, leave the convent and marry.

After the *Alteratie* of 1578 (see Amstelkring Museum) when Catholic institutions were taken over by Protestants, the Beguines were allowed to continue their work of education, caring for the poor and nursing the sick. They could only worship in secret, however, and a clandestine chapel, the Begijnhofkapel, was built in 1671, hidden behind the domestic façade of no 30. The chapel can be visited; its entrance is opposite the former convent church, handed over to Scottish Presbyterians in 1607 and subsequently renamed the Engelsekerk, the English Church. This was rebuilt in 1727 and a more recent addition is the pulpit, with panels designed by Mondrian. As well as remaining the main church of Amsterdam's British community, the Engelsekerk hosts a series of free lunchtime concerts in July and August and evening concerts during the rest of the year (details posted at the church door).

Many of the buildings of the Begijnhof were 'modernised' by the addition of new façades in the 17th and 18th centuries. The last of the Beguines died in 1971 and the houses are now let, for a nominal rent, to elderly women and female students.

Entrance at Spui no 14 or from the Amsterdam Historical Museum
Open: daily from dawn to dusk;
Begijnhofkapel open daily 9am–5pm;

Engelsekerk open only for concerts (see above) and for services on Sunday at 10.30am. Admission free
Trams 1, 2, 4, 5, 9, 16, 24 or 25
Nearby: Amsterdam Historical Museum.

BIJBELS MUSEUM (BIBLICAL MUSEUM)

This specialised collection is devoted to the history of the Old and New Testaments and is an important research centre for Jewish and Christian scholars. The displays illustrate life in biblical times through archaeological material and reconstructions of key buildings, such as the Temple of Solomon. For many visitors the appeal is the house itself, with its stately period details and ceiling paintings by Jacob van Wit.

The house is part of a row (nos 362 to 328) designed in 1662 by Philips Vingboons, one of the leading architects of the Golden Age. The builder was Jacob Cromhout who lived at no 366, hence its alternative name, the Cromhouthuizen. Cromhout's trademark, a crooked stick, appears on a plaque on the façade.

Herengracht 366 (tel: 624 2436)
Open: Tuesday to Saturday 10am–5pm; Sunday and public holidays 1pm–5pm (closed Monday, 1 January and 30 April) Admission charge.
Trams 1, 2, or 5
Nearby: Begijnhof.

BEURS VAN BERLAGE

Amsterdam's Beurs, the former Stock Exchange, was reopened as a cultural centre in 1988 and is worth visiting for concerts given by The Netherlands Philharmonic and Chamber orchestras and as an architectural spectacle in its own right. The Beurs was rebuilt in 1903 by Hendrick Petrus Berlage, the

Inside the Beurs van Berlage

best Dutch architect of his age, in an imaginative style that anticipates the work of the 1930s Amsterdam School (see Spaarndammerburt). The superb interiors are a *tour de force* of patterned brickwork and colourful tiles under a glass and wrought-iron roof.

Damrak 277 (tel: 626 5257 general enquiries: 627 0466 box office)
Open: the building is not open in the normal way; it is best seen by joining a guided architectural tour run by Archivise (tel: 625·8908), by visiting the café (Grand Café Beurs van Berlage), which is decorated with tile murals of Dutch industry, or by attending a concert.

Canal Life

Canals give Amsterdam its distinctive character, but it is a mistake to call the city the 'Venice of the North'. Amsterdammers are proud that their city is a vital, living place – to them Venice is a dead city, a theme park abandoned to tourism.

Swans, ducks and fish have returned to the canals following a 10-year clean-up campaign.

Dredgers keep the canal bottoms clear of debris – everything from abandoned bicycles to the cars of careless drivers who ended up in the water.

Until the IJsselmeer was dammed, the canals were flushed twice daily by natural tidal flow. Now a complex system of sluices and mechanical pumps does the job instead. Every night a third of the

By the time Amsterdam's great phase of canal-building ended in the 17th century, there were 100 islands and 400 bridges. Today the canals are quiet backwaters where people relax on their houseboats, take strolls, and simply stare into the water

water in the canals is replaced by fresh water from the IJsselmeer. Excess water can also be pumped out if flood waters threaten the city after heavy rain.

There are 160 separate canals in the city – totalling 75km in length – spanned by 1,281 bridges, many of which are illuminated at night. Most bridges are fixed but several old wooden drawbridges remain, like the Magerebrug across the Amstel, topped by huge wooden balance beams that enable the central portion to be raised to admit tall-masted boats.

About 5,000 people in Amsterdam live in a total of 2,400 boats. These range from lovingly restored barges, gaily painted and bright with rooftop gardens, to utilitarian floating sheds.

Living on a canal boat is not cheap; the cost of a boat and mooring is about the same as the rent for an equivalent sized flat, but for boat dwellers it is a deliberately chosen way of life. Some Amsterdammers consider the canals a wasted asset since little use is made of their transport potential. Perhaps this situation will change if the city ever gets round to banning the automobile.

Churches

*W*hile all sorts of fringe religions flourish in Amsterdam, from Hare Krishna to New Age anthroposophy, conventional church-going has declined, leaving many of the city's churches forlorn, locked and redundant. The three main churches can be visited, however, and all of them are monuments of significant historical and architectural importance worthy of the city's reverance.

The imposing façade of Oude Kerk

NIEUWE KERK (NEW CHURCH)

The Nieuwe Kerk, on Dam square, is now run by a foundation whose policy is to put the church to a wide variety of uses, including art exhibitions, concerts, lectures and even antiques fairs. Even so, it remains the national church of The Netherlands, used for the investiture of monarchs, as when Queen Beatrix was enthroned in 1980. The church was first built in 1408 – it is 'new' only in the sense that it is 200 years younger than the Oude Kerk (Old Church). It was gutted by fire in 1645, hence all its furnishings date from the Golden Age. These include a fine baroque pulpit of 1649 carved by Aelbert Vinckenbrink with figures of the Evangelists, Faith, Hope, Charity, Justice and Prudence; a magnificent organ case designed by the architect Jacob van Campen, an ornate bronze choir screen and elegant wooden pews. Several national heroes are commemorated, including Admiral Michiel de Ruyter (died 1676) whose magnificent monument dominates the choir.

Dam square Open: daily 11am–5pm (conditionally)
Admission free but charges apply for exhibitions, recitals and other events
Trams 1, 2, 4, 5, 9, 13, 14, 16, 17, 24 , 25 or buses 18, 21, 22
Nearby: Koninklijk Paleis.

OUDE KERK (OLD CHURCH)

The city's oldest church, still in use for services, was founded in the early 13th century and retains its medieval atmosphere. Pictures of ships feature everywhere, reminding us that the church is dedicated to St Nicolaas, the patron saint of sailors; ships feature on the painted wooden ceiling vault and on the choir stalls, in the form of graffiti scratched by bored churchgoers. The nave is ringed by numerous chapels sponsored by the city's powerful trade guilds. Richly coloured stained glass in the north choir, dating from 1555, depicts the Life of the Virgin. The tower has an especially tuneful carillon of bells, made in the 17th century, which is played every Saturday between 4pm and 5pm and it is possible to climb the spire for sweeping views over the port and city.

Ouderkerksplein 23
Open: church April to October, Monday to Saturday 11am–5pm, Sunday 1.30pm–5pm; November to March, Monday to Saturday 1pm–3pm, Sunday 1.30pm–3pm. Tower 1 June to September, Monday and Thursday 2pm–5pm, Tuesday and Wednesday 11am–2pm
Admission charge to the tower
Trams 4, 9, 16, 24 or 25
Nearby: Amstelkring Museum.

WESTERKERK (WEST CHURCH)

Westerkerk, built by Hendrik de Keyser in the early 17th century, when the canal circle was first laid out, is renowned for two things: Rembrandt's grave and the lofty tower. Rembrandt was buried in an unmarked pauper's grave whose location was rediscovered by archaeologists during recent restoration work. The tower, which can be climbed, is the tallest in Amsterdam at 83m. It is topped by the gold, red and blue crown of the Habsburg Holy Roman Emperor, Maximilian I. The city gained the right to display the imperial crown in its coat of arms in 1489. According to one story, the privilege was granted after Maximilian I was miraculously cured of an illness having visited Amsterdam's shrine of the Sacred Host. Others, more cynically, say that Maximilian gave away his crown – at least symbolically – as a measure of his indebtedness to Amsterdam's bankers.

Prinsengracht 281, corner of Westermarkt
Open: church May to 12 September Monday to Saturday, 10am–4pm. Tower June to September, Tuesday, Wednesday, Friday and Saturday 2pm–5pm
Admission charge to the tower
Trams 13, 14 ,17 or bus 21
Nearby: Anne Frankhuis

Westerkerk with its gold-topped tower

The world-famous auditorium of the Concertgebouw

CONCERTGEBOUW

Johannes Brahms, who conducted his Third Symphony in Amsterdam in 1879, is reputed to have told his hosts: 'You are good people but bad musicians'. The remark spurred the city to set about creating a permanent orchestra and concert hall, both of which have since achieved worldwide acclaim. The Concertgebouw building is renowned for its acoustics and ranks as one of the top three concert halls in the world, alongside Vienna and Boston. The imposing building was designed by A van Gendt and opened in 1888, an elegant neo-classical structure decorated with reliefs of the Muses and celestial musicians. Following subsidence, the building was restored for its centenary in 1988, and given a controversial new glass foyer.

The resident orchestra, the Concertgebouworkest, achieved international renown under Willem Mengelberg and Bernard Haitink; now it is conducted by Riccardo Chailly. Other top orchestras perform here and the busy concert programme sometimes includes jazz as well as classics.

Concertgebouwplein 2–6
(tel: 671 8345 box office)
Open: the main focus of architectural interest is the exterior, which can be seen at any time; the best way to see the interior is to attend one of the numerous concerts, including free lunchtime recitals given on Wednesdays. The box office is open Monday to Friday 10am–5pm
Trams 3, 5, 12 or 16
Nearby: Rijksmuseum, Stedelijk Museum, Rijksmuseum Vincent Van Gogh.

ELECTRISCHE MUSEUMTRAMLIJN (ELECTRIC TRAMLINE MUSEUM)

The trams that provide an efficient public transport system in the centre of Amsterdam seem to belong to another age, with their old-fashioned streetcar design and jangling bells. They are, however, youngsters compared to the 60 or so historic trams that have been gathered together from all over Europe to create this transport museum, which is understandably popular with children. Most of the trams are static but some are used on summer Sundays to provide a service from Haarlemermeer station to Amsterdamse Bos (Amsterdam Wood). Here you can alight for a picnic, a walk or a visit to the playground, farm reserve or Bosmuseum (Woodland Museum). Alternatively you can continue on through the 800 hectare park to the tram

Outside the Concertgebouw

terminus at Amstelveen, a total journey time of 30 minutes.

Haarlemermeer station, Amstelveenseweg 264 (tel: 673 7538)
Open: 1 April to 31 October, Sunday 10.30am–6pm. Trams depart every 20 minutes. Also, in July and August, trams operate on Tuesday, Wednesday, Thursday and Saturday at 1pm, 2.15pm and 3.30pm
Admission charge
Trams 6 or 16
Nearby: Amsterdamse Bos
*(see **Getting away from it all**).*

World-class music on offer

HEINEKEN BRAUWERIJ

A trip to the Heineken Brewery Museum is more than just an indulgence for beer lovers; the former brewery, closed in 1988, has been turned into an excellent museum that reveals often surprising facts about the social history of brewing and beer consumption. The museum charts the invention of beer by the ancient Sumerians, the origins of the first taverns and beer halls in Germany, the role of beer in carnival festivities as depicted in the paintings of the Brueghels and the vital importance of beer taxes to Amsterdam's medieval

Heavy horses at the Heineken Museum

economy; vast quantities were consumed at the time simply because beer was a safer drink than water. Various parts of the brewing process are explained by audio-visual displays and the traditional white-tiled brewhouse, with its vast gleaming copper vats, is kept as spotless as it was when the brewery was in operation.

Heineken finally closed its Amsterdam brewery in 1988 and relocated to new plants at Den Bosch and Zouterwoude. It was a sad day for Amsterdam as beer had been brewed on the premises since 1592. The present firm was founded in 1864 by Gerard Adriaan Heineken and its products have become a household name in many parts of the world. Closure was inevitable because the Amsterdam plant could only produce 80,000 bottles of lager an hour – a lot of beer but less than Amsterdam alone consumes. The new plants have a staggering combined capacity of more than 1 million bottles an hour.
Stadhouderskade 78 (tel: 523 9239)
Open: guided tours at 9am, 9.45am and 10.30am Monday to Friday; 15 May to 15 September 1pm, 1.45pm, and 2.30pm also). Each tour lasts around two hours. Closed holidays
Admission charge
Trams 6, 7, 10, 16, 24 or 25
Nearby: Albert Cuypstraat (see **Markets***).*

JOODS HISTORISCH MUSEUM (JEWISH HISTORICAL MUSEUM)

This museum is devoted to the history of the Jews in Amsterdam, a tragic story curtailed by the Nazi persecution of World War II. However, the museum is at pains to stress the continuity of Jewish life in The Netherlands and it seeks to explain Jewish culture in general.

The museum is housed in the former

Ashkenazic synagogue complex, a series of 17th- and 18th-century buildings, and the displays cover three main themes. The first is concerned with the terror and persecution of the war, brought vividly to life by contemporary photographs and the personal accounts of survivors. The second explains the Jewish religion, the major events in the calendar, its rituals and laws on diet and hygiene. Finally there is an account of the Jewish contribution to public life, politics and industry in Amsterdam, especially in developing the diamond industry.

The collection takes time to absorb, leaving visitors sober and reflective, but there is a lighter note – the excellent kosher café serves Dutch Jewish specialities such as almond *bolus* and ginger-flavoured *boterkoek*, buttercake.
Jonas Daniel Meyerplein 2–4
(tel: 626 9945)
Open: daily 11am–5pm
(closed Yom Kippur)
Admission charge
Trams 9 or 14
Nearby: Rembrandthuis

KROMHOUT MUSEUM

The Kromhout Works is the only remaining shipyard of the many that once filled Amsterdam's eastern harbour. Today it concentrates on restoring historic vessels. The shipyard was founded in the 18th century by Diede Jansen Kromhout and specialised in building iron vessels in the 19th century. The ornate glass and iron canopy that stands over the original slipway now shelters the working part of the museum where visitors can watch boats and engines being repaired. The adjoining display area features models of steamers, shipwrights' tools and

A sea-dog's paradise at the Kromhout Museum

engravings of the docks in their heyday, crowded with tall-masted ships and bustling with activity.
Hoogte Kadijk 147 (tel: 627 6777)
Open: Monday to Friday 9am–4pm, also
Saturday and Sunday in summer,
12 noon–5pm
Admission charge
Buses 22 or 28
Nearby: Scheepvaart (Maritime) Museum,
*Docklands (see **Walk 10**).*

Jewish Amsterdam

When Amsterdam was liberated from Nazi occupation on 5 May 1945, the city's Jewish population had fallen from 140,000 to less than 45,000. The survivors had lost everything – family, friends and homes. These stark facts are brought home by a visit to Jodenbuurt, the former Jewish Quarter, where only a handful of pre-war buildings remain.

Among the first refugees to arrive in Amsterdam at the beginning of the 17th century were Sephardic Jews from Spain and Portugal. They built the huge Portuguese Synagogue that dominates Mr Visserplein, dating from 1671. Ashkenazic Jews from Germany and Poland soon followed; their synagogue complex on Jonas Daniel Meyerplein now houses the Jewish Historical Museum.

The statue of a burly dockworker stands between these two buildings. It was sculpted in 1952 by Marie Andriessen to commemorate a brave and singular act of defiance; in February 1941 the city's dockers and transport workers led a general strike in protest against Nazi treatment of the Jews. The strike, brutally suppressed, has gone down in Dutch history as the city's 'day beyond praise'.

Placenames in the area perpetuate the memory of prominent Jews. Mr Visser was President of the Supreme Court of The Netherlands until dismissed by the Nazis; he played a prominent role in the Resistance until he died of natural causes. Jonas Daniel Meyer was a prominent 19th-century lawyer and a lifelong campaigner for Jewish civil rights.

Despite everything, Jews still play an important role in the city's life. The van Moppes family sought refuge in Brazil during the war. They later returned to found one of the city's best-known diamond companies, the flourishing firm of A van Moppes & Zoon (see **Diamonds**).

Street sign in the Jewish Quarter

*Visitors to the
Jewish Historical Museum
find a living exhibition of Jewish
faith and history*

Koninklijk Paleis (Royal Palace)

The Royal Palace, on Dam square, is Amsterdam's most prestigious architectural monument. It was built as an expression of civic pride between 1648 and 1655, when Amsterdam was at the peak of its power as a maritime trading city, capital of an empire stretching from the Americas to Australia.

Originally built as the Stadhuis or Town Hall, it was the one flamboyant structure in a city characterised by architectural restraint. There were practical reasons why Amsterdam had so few grandiose public buildings of any size: the soggy subsoil of mud and silt simply could not support any great weight of masonry.

The architect, Jacob van Campen, had to overcome this technical difficulty before he could fulfil his commission, to design the biggest town hall in all of Europe. He did so by creating a solid

The figure of Atlas above the Royal Palace

raft of timber piles, each 18m deep. The precise number of the piles – 13,659 – is known to every Amsterdam schoolchild because of a simple formula: to the number of days in the year (365) add 1 in front and 9 behind.

On top of this raft, van Campen built the huge neo-classical edifice whose main façades are 80m long - just 2.13m more than the town hall of Antwerp, up to then the biggest in Europe. Amsterdam further signalled its supremacy over Antwerp, the city that had once been its major rival in the competition for maritime trade, by placing the figure of Atlas holding up the globe on the west front pediment; below all the nations of the world are depicted offering up their goods to an allegorical female figure representing the city of Amsterdam. By contrast, the weathervane on top of the central cupola depicts the humble *Dutch Koggeschip* – the Dutch Cog – one of thousands of sturdy merchant ships that roamed the

world bringing back the spices and tropical produce that made the city so immensely rich.

A notable feature of the Stadhuis is the lack of a formal entrance; puzzled visitors often wander round the block several times before discovering the small concealed doorway (on the right-hand side of the portico facing on to Dam square). Again there were good reasons for this: the old city hall had been stormed by rioting Anabaptists in 1535 declaring the imminent end of the world. Strikes and demonstrations were a regular feature of city life. The basement of the town hall also contained the city's prison, arsenal and bank vaults – according to the historian Mark Girouard, up to 16 million Dutch florins could be stored in the vault at any one time, 'a foundation every bit as impressive as the famous 13,659 timber piles'. For all these reasons the town hall had to be impregnable and the entrance was therefore built deliberately small.

On the other hand the Stadhuis was a public building, open to anyone who cared to enter. The ground floor housed the courts and council chamber as well as the offices of various city charities responsible for managing orphanages and hospitals. The upstairs was largely empty. In their desire for the biggest and best, Amsterdammers got more space than they could actually use.

In 1808 Napoleon invaded The Netherlands and put his brother on the throne. The Stadhuis was turned into the royal palace of today. As a result the rooms contain an extensive collection of Empire furniture, but the most striking feature is the wealth of 17th-century marble sculpture, the work of Artus Quellin. The sculpture is allegorical, indicating the use of each hall: Justice,

Guards on ceremonial duty outside the palace

Wisdom and Mercy decorate the tribunal or main courtroom; Venus is found in the room where marriages were registered and Icarus, falling from the sky, in the office where merchants filed for bankruptcy. These playful and imaginative figures contrast with the more ponderous paintings that decorate the walls and ceilings, but even these provide an insight into key moments in the city's history and the moral values of the Golden Age.

Dam square (tel: 624 8698 extension 217)
Open: mid-June to 1 September daily 1pm–5pm; guided tours take place during this period at 1.30pm on Wednesdays; out of season group tours can be arranged by ringing the above number (minimum 10 people)
Admission charge
Trams 1, 2, 4, 9, 13, 14, 16, 17, 24 or 25
Nearby: Nieuwe Kerk (see **Churches**).

KINDERMUSEUM TM JUNIOR

TM Junior is a separate branch of the Tropenmuseum (Tropical Museum) which mounts special exhibitions for children and an imaginative range of hands-on workshop activities. The aim is to introduce young people to different cultures and ways of life. For example, young people learn about life in Senegal by exploring a reconstruction of a tribal hut, hearing stories, watching films, learning dances, playing drums and cooking a rice-based meal – and by meeting and talking to Senegalese children.

These events are ideally suited to children aged six to 12 and the numbers are limited, so it is best to book in advance – checking, too, whether the event is suitable for children who do not speak Dutch. And, of course, your children do not have to attend a workshop; the exhibitions themselves are fun and educational in their own right. Parents are admitted – provided that each adult is accompanied by at least one child.

Linnaeusstraat 2 (tel: 568 8300/8295)
Open: term-time, Sunday 12 noon–4pm;
school holidays, Monday to Friday 11am–
4pm, Sunday 12 noon–4pm (children aged
6–12 only)
Admission charge
Trams 9, 10, 14 or bus 22
Nearby: Tropenmuseum.

MADAME TUSSAUD SCENERAMA

If the Amsterdam Historical Museum is too dry for your tastes, try learning about the Golden Age of The Netherlands through the waxworks and tableaux of Madame Tussaud. In a swift romp through the 17th century you will meet William of Orange and watch

Rembrandt at work in Madame Tussaud's

Rembrandt at work in his studio; enter a merchant's house, modelled on a painting by Vermeeer, and watch children skating on the frozen canals of Amsterdam. Then the scene changes and you are back in the 20th century witnessing the first Moon walk and meeting famous politicians, pop stars and royalty. The wax figures move, you can watch yourself on TV shaking hands with world leaders and the special effects are laid on thick – all good fun if it is a cold, wet day or your children are bored with art and architecture.

Peek & Cloppenburg Department Store,
Dam 20 (tel: 622 9949)
Open: daily 10am–5.30pm (closed 30 April
and 25 December)
Admission charge
Trams 1, 2, 4, 9, 13, 14, 16, 17, 24 or 25
Nearby: Koninklijk Paleis, Nieuwe Kerk
*(see **Churches**), Amsterdam Historical*
Museum.

MUSEUM FODOR
(MODERN ART MUSEUM)

From the outside the Fodor Museum is an over-ornate Victorian building, dating from 1861. Inside, by contrast, the spacious rooms are starkly modern as befits a museum whose role is to act as a showcase for the contemporary arts. The Fodor Museum is linked to the bigger Stedelijk Museum and sometimes displays new acquisitions or material from reserve collections. Most of the time, however, its changing exhibitions feature new work by local artists, ranging from bookbindings and poetry to video productions; the attractive garden is often used as an outdoor sculpture gallery and there is a well-stocked bookshop specialising in modern art.

Keizersgracht 609 (tel: 624 9919)
Open: daily 11am–5pm, but phone to check since reconstruction work began in 1991 (closed 1 January)
Admission charge
Trams 16, 24 or 25
Nearby: Van Loon Museum, Willet-Holthuysen Museum.

NMB-POSTBANK BUILDING

The head office of the NMB-PostBank, the fourth biggest bank in The Netherlands, is an intriguing and imaginative building, worth seeking out in its suburban location by those interested in new architectural trends. The building, the most expensive ever built in The Netherlands, was completed in 1987. It was designed by Ton Alberts and Max van Huut in accordance with anthroposophical principles, a New Age philosophy in vogue with Amsterdam intellectuals that has been described as combining western humanist values with elements from eastern religions.

The building is designed to be 'organic'; none of the walls meet at right angles, a rejection of the alienating box-like form of most office blocks. Critics describe the result as a giant sandcastle – admirers compare it to ancient Inca architecture. Running water is a major feature – the sound of waterfalls and fountains intended to have a calming effect – and there are numerous courtyard gardens. The building is also a model of energy efficiency.

The NMB-PostBank building stands in ironic counterpoint to the nearby towerblocks of Bijlmermeer, themselves the result of architectural experimentation in the 1960s. These stark, utilitarian buildings, designed to the principles of Le Corbusier, house a population of some 35,000 Surinamese, immigrants from the former Dutch colony in South America, hence Bijlmermeer has been called the biggest Surinamese 'city' outside the Americas.

Bijlmermeerplein 888 (tel: 563 9111)
Open: Monday to Friday 9am–4pm; the above telelphone number can be used to book group tours, but there is a long waiting list
Admission free
Buses 59, 60, 61, 62 or 137; Metro station Bullewijk

NMB-Postbank Building

Rembrandthuis
(Museum Het)

The house in which Rembrandt spent the happiest and most successful years of his life is now a museum used to display an almost complete set of his etchings – 245 out of the 280 he is known to have made – along with drawings, personal memorabilia and period furniture. One room has an exhibition explaining the techniques of engraving and the walls are also hung with paintings by Rembrandt's pupils and by his teacher, Pieter Lastman.

Inside Rembrandt's house

The handsome Renaissance house was built in 1606. Rembrandt bought it in 1639, when he was 33 years of age. He had previously lodged in the same street, having moved to Amsterdam from his native Leiden in 1631. He soon became an acclaimed artist, able to count on an income from major commissions. Even so, he borrowed heavily to buy, furnish and maintain the house. This, and his lack of business acumen, contributed to his bankruptcy. In 1658 his creditors forced him to sell the house, though he was allowed to continue living in it until 1660, when he moved to a cheaper home in the Jordaan district.

The house remains as it was in Rembrandt's day; the only subsequent change was the addition of a third storey with a classical pediment in place of the original step gable. Rembrandt and his household lived on the ground floor; the first floor served as his studio and the attic as the studio of his pupils.

The house was then located on the edge of the city, in the fast-growing Jewish Quarter. Rembrandt chose the situation because the countryside was not far away.

The streets of the Jewish Quarter provided Rembrandt with a constant source of inspiration. His affection for low-life characters can be seen in the famous series of engravings, hung in this museum, of beggars, vagabonds, organ-grinders and rat-catchers – he even portrayed himself in the guise of a beggar.

Among the other pictures displayed are views of Amsterdam and the surrounding countryside, several revealing self-portraits, and etchings of the artist's parents, his wife and their son, Titus. A visit to the toilets is a must just for Rembrandt's drawings of a woman squatting in the bushes and a man standing in a pose of evident relief!

Jodenbreestraat 4–6 (tel: 624 9486)
Open: Monday to Saturday 10am–5pm,
Sunday and public holidays 1pm–5pm
(closed 1 January)
Admission charge
Trams 9 or 14
Nearby: Jewish Historical Museum.

REMBRANDT'S LIFE

Rembrandt van Rijn was born in Leiden in 1606, the eighth child of a prosperous corn miller who owned a mill close to the River Rhine, hence the family name. Rembrandt was destined for a career in the law until he gave up university to concentrate on art. He moved to Amsterdam in 1631 and the following year received his first major commission, *The Anatomy Lesson of Dr Tulp* (now in the Mauritshuis Museum, Den Haag) portraying members of the city's guild of surgeons.

Fame and fortune followed, but so did personal tragedy. His wife, Saskia, died in 1642; three of their four children died in early childhood, leaving only Titus, whom Rembrandt adored. In that same year, despite Saskia's death, Rembrandt painted his best-known picture, *The Night Watch.*

This occupies the position of honour in the Rijksmuseum, but it was criticised in its time because some faces in the picture are partially hidden – the realism we value was condemned at the time and his critics further accused Rembrandt of not following the 'rules of art', instead pursuing his own private insights.

He began to receive fewer commissions and, in 1660, forced into bankruptcy, moved to a modest dwelling in Jordaan. Here he painted some of his greatest works, including the glowing and mysterious *Jewish Bride* (Rijksmuseum). The sickly Titus died, aged 27, in 1668 and Rembrandt followed him less than a year later. In October 1669 he was buried in an unmarked pauper's grave in Westerkerk, an ignominious end for a man who is now regarded as one of the greatest artists of all time.

Rembrandt's vibrant genius revealed in The Nightwatch

Rijksmuseum I

*T*he Rijksmuseum is one of Amsterdam's major highlights. The museum building is a vast neo-gothic palace with Burgundian towers and sculptural reliefs, designed by P J H Cuypers and completed in 1885. It houses the national art collection of The Netherlands - a treasure-house of paintings, applied art, porcelain, silver and Asiatic sculpture. The museum is far too big to absorb in one visit: it pays to be selective and visitors with a Museum Card (see Practical Guide) can return as many times as they like without charge.

Free leaflets showing the layout of the museum are available in the entrance foyer. The museum shop also sells a range of inexpensive and user-friendly *Viewfinder* guides which send visitors on a 30-minute trail through the warren of rooms in pursuit of particular themes - *How paintings tell stories,* for example, on narrative art, and *How many hairs are there on a dog?* on realism in art. Finally there is an informative audio-visual introduction to the art of the Golden Age, with commentaries in several languages, shown at approximately 20-minute intervals in the first-floor film theatre.

Rembrandt

For many visitors the Rijksmuseum means one painting, Rembrandt's celebrated *Night Watch.* It can be seen by heading straight up to the first floor where the huge canvas is given pride of place at the end of the Gallery of Honour, in room 224. *The Night Watch* was named in the 19th century when experts believed the painting depicted a night scene. The layers of soot-blackened varnish have since been removed to reveal a quite different picture in which Rembrandt's dramatic use of sunlight and shade can be fully appreciated. Despite restoration, the old name has stuck, partly because the now-accepted title, *The Militia Company of Captain Frans Banning Cocq,* is such a mouthful.

The painting is an official portrait of one of the militia companies which acted as a combined police force–cum–army, ensuring law and order in the city and taking it in turns to mount a guard at the city gates. Each company had its own clubhouse and wealthier members paid for group portraits to adorn the walls. Hundreds of such portraits – the equivalent of today's group photographs – have survived, including those that hang in the Civic Guard Gallery of the Amsterdam Historical Museum.

A close look at masterpieces in the Rijksmuseum

Rembrandt's innovation was to break away from the static banquet scene or formal pose to show the militia company in action. Captain Cocq is giving his men the order to set off on a patrol of duty. He and his lieutenant are lit by a pool of sunlight while the militiamen behind are shown emerging from the shadowy gate of their clubhouse. The painting is full of movement as the men shoulder their weapons and form up into marching line, the dynamism enhanced by the play of light and the little girl caught up in the disorder. Her presence in the picture is a mystery; it is suggested that she may have been the daughter of the landlord of the militia clubhouse. The dead rooster hanging from her belt is an enigmatic pun (perhaps with bawdy connotations) on the name of Captain Cocq.

Rembrandt's contemporaries were not universally impressed by this work; some hailed it as a masterpiece of realism but far more censured him for failing in his fundamental duty as a portraitist to show the faces of each militiaman clearly. Instead, several faces are obscured by gesturing arms or shadow.

To the left of *The Night Watch*, rooms 220 to 223 contain further Rembrandt works, including two self-portraits – one painted at the age of 22, the other *(Self-Portrait as the Apostle Paul)* in 1661 after bankruptcy had forced a major change in his lifestyle. In the same year he painted the arresting *Bridal Pair*, also known as *The Jewish Bride,* a tender portrait of an unknown couple in glowing and heavily impasted reds and golds. Near by is another masterpiece – *De Staalmeesters.* This depicts five inspectors of the Drapers' Guild and a hatless servant. From the way they look

An outside view of the Rijksmuseum

out of the picture it has been suggested that they are portrayed at a public meeting – someone in the invisible audience has addressed an unexpected question to them and their expressions, brilliantly highlighted by the muted black of their clothes, range from bemused tolerance to a rather lofty contempt.

Stadhouderskade 42 (tel: 673 2121)
Open: Tuesday to Saturday 10am–5pm,
Sunday and public holidays 1pm–5pm
(closed Monday and 1 January)
Admission charge
Trams 6, 7, 10, 16, 24 or 25
Nearby: Van Gogh Museum,
Stedelijk Museum.

Rijksmuseum II

The Golden Age

Apart from the works of Rembrandt the Rijksmuseum is noted for its collection of 17th-century works painted during the period of peace and prosperity known as the Golden Age of The Netherlands. They are displayed in rooms 209 to 222, beginning with the lively portrait of *Isaac Massa and his Wife,* by Frans Hals. In this genial picture, the tubby and prosperous Isaac Massa leans back as if to show off his neat smiling wife, a paragon of fidelity as symbolised by the ivy clinging to the tree behind.

Hendrick Avercamp's *Winter Landscape* in the same room and Jacob van Ruysdael's *Mill at Wijk by Duursteede* in room 214 are superb examples of the

Avercamp's Winter Landscape

landscape painting for which Dutch artists are renowned.

Room 216 is devoted to the witty genre paintings of Jan Steen. Many of them depict the artist himself and his family in scenes of wild abandon, illustrating popular moralistic proverbs of the age – for example, *homo bulla,* or 'man is a bubble'. At first sight *The Merry Family* looks like a happy domestic scene until you notice that the children are smoking, drinking and being as licentious as their parents. The motto above the fireplace provides an ironic commentary; it says the young will sing the same old song, meaning that parents should beware of setting a bad example.

Quite different in tone altogether are the exquisite works of the Delft School hung in room 222, including four paintings by Vermeer and several by

Pieter de Hooch. These simple paintings radiate peace and tranquillity, lending spiritual significance to the dutiful performance of the most ordinary domestic activities.

Dutch History and Asiatic Art

Rooms 101 to 114, on the ground floor, are used to display works that illustrate important aspects of Dutch history, even though they have no special artistic merit. They include portraits of key figures, such as William of Orange, historic battles at sea and on land, scenes of everyday life in the 17th century and, most fascinating of all, relics of colonial life in the East Indies, Ceylon, China and Japan.

From here it makes sense to continue the theme by descending to the Asiatic art collection in the basement, rooms 11 to 23. Here, among Indonesian sculptures and Hindu-Javanese architectural fragments, is the arresting figure of *Shiva, Lord of the Dance,* surrounded by a ring of fire. This 12th-century bronze from southern India is as stunning a work in its own way as the paintings upstairs, yet it receives far fewer visitors. The section ends with a comprehensive display of Chinese ceramics and some beautifully embroidered Japanese textiles.

Sculpture and Applied Art

This collection is organised chronologically, beginning with medieval and Renaissance art on the top floor, rooms 238 to 261. Some of the best exhibits consist of Romanesque and Gothic sculpture rescued from various abbeys and churches in The Netherlands. For fans of Delftware, rooms 255 to 257 contain a wealth of examples, including novelty items such

The distinctive blue and white of exquisite Delftware

as a birdcage, a violin and a pair of high-heeled shoes.

From room 261 a staircase leads to the ground floor where you may have to queue to get close to the popular doll's houses in room 162, made in the 18th century with exquisite attention to detail. The remaining rooms (162 to 181) illustrate Dutch interior design in the 18th and 19th centuries. This theme continues in the little visited basement (rooms 24 to 34) which is well worth seeking out for its outstanding collection of Empire and art nouveau furniture.

Later Dutch Art

Paintings of the 18th to the early 20th century are displayed in Rooms 134 to 149, in the ground floor Drucker Extension. Most rewarding are the Impressionistic works of The Hague and Amsterdam Schools hung in the last three rooms – notably the atmospheric pictures of Amsterdam street life at the turn of the century painted by George Hendrick Breitner.

Art in the Golden Age

John Evelyn, Samuel Pepys and other visitors to 17th-century Amsterdam were amazed by the quantity of fine art on sale in the city. Amsterdam developed the first truly open market for art, which was sold through dealers, bookshops and auctioneers. Instead of art being the preserve of rich patrons and institutions, ordinary citizens could commission portraits of their houses, possessions, friends or even of their prize animals (see Paulus Potter's *The Young Bull* in the Mauritshuis Museum, Den Haag).

Amsterdammers seem to have been particularly fond of paintings with a coded message. Understanding the symbolism reveals that many of the Rijksmuseum's pictures are far more complex than they seem on the surface.

Dogs, for example, represent gluttony and licentiousness, reflecting on the behaviour of the people in the picture. Golden vases, cut-glass decanters, musical instruments and peacock's feathers represent vanity. The frailty of human fortune is symbolised by eggshells or a fallen glass. Sometimes the paintings contain verbal puns: *vogolen*, the word for a dead bird, is similar to the slang term for copulation, hence a man

holding up a dead pheasant is saying more than you might at first suspect.

The paintings of the age therefore work in two ways; as representations of everyday life and as serious moral works. Jan Steen's bawdy tavern scenes in the Rijksmuseum are a warning against loose morals. Another of his works in the same museum has an innocuous title – *The Toilet* – yet it is full of erotic allusions: the candlestick, the sleeping dog, the red stockings, symbol of a prostitute, and the open jewellery box. Literate Amsterdammers, whilst enjoying the painting as a piece of erotica, would know well how to read this as a warning against the prostitution of moral principles for mercenary ends.

Jan Steen's Two Kinds of Games

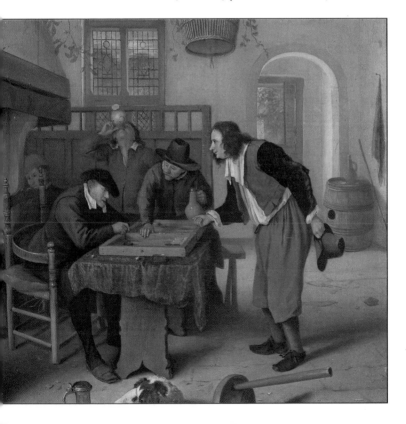

Rijksmuseum Vincent van Gogh

*F*rom the outside the Van Gogh Museum, designed by Gerrit Rietveld and completed in 1973, is a stark and unwelcoming building. Inside the huge whitewashed walls glow with the intense colours of Van Gogh's canvases. The collection, comprising some 200 paintings and over 600 drawings, was bequeathed to the city of Amsterdam by Van Gogh's nephew, also called Vincent. A selection of this work is displayed on the first floor while the rest of the museum is used for temporary exhibitions that throw light on Van Gogh's achievement by comparison with the work of his friends and contemporaries.

Van Gogh's work is presented in chronological order, begining with his early studies of peasant life. These were painted in 1884–5 when Van Gogh was living at the family rectory in Nuenen, a village in Noord Brabant province surrounded by peat moorland. The colours of the soil are reflected in these sombre sketches of coarse faces and rough hands. *The Potato Eaters,* an early masterpiece, still has an arresting force, though Van Gogh explained, in a letter to his brother Theo, that he did not intend to present rural life as brutalised and backward; 'I have tried to make it clear', he wrote, 'that those people,

eating their potatoes in the lamplight, have dug the earth with those very hands they put in the dish, and so it speaks of manual labour, and how they have honestly earned their food.'

The next section covers Van Gogh's time in Paris (1886–8) and his various experiments with *pointillisme* and the light airy style of the Impressionists. Van Gogh soon tired of city life and the next section, covering his period in Arles (1888–9) shows a sudden transformation in his work. The paintings of this period are extraordinarily vivid and intense, and

View on Arles by Vincent van Gogh

VAN GOGH THE MISFIT

Van Gogh's artistic career lasted a mere 10 years, yet he painted over 2,000 works – 200 alone in the 15 months he spent in Arles. Painting was a passion ('one works without being aware', he wrote) and he would even work all night with candles stuck around the rim of his hat.

Van Gogh sold only one painting in his life; he was so poor that his diet consisted of meagre amounts of bread and more copious amounts of coffee and alcohol. Chronic undernourishment and lack of sleep may have contributed to his mental breakdown. In a famous quarrel he threatened his friend Guigin with a knife and then, in a fit of remorse, cut off his own ear. He admitted himself to an asylum but not long afterwards, aged 37, he shot himself. Only after his death were his talents appreciated. The misfit artist, who saw himself as a failure, now commands world-record auction prices and he is, judging by the millions of reproductions of his work that are now sold every year, by far the world's most popular painter.

the colours are stunning – the blazing yellows and oranges of _Sunflowers,_ the brilliant white of peach blossom against a turquoise spring sky, the blues and yellows of harvest scenes and landscapes all speak of Van Gogh's enthusiasm for 'the full effect of colour'.

The two final sections of the museum show the pictures he produced while staying at the St Remy asylum (1889–90), after the famous ear-cutting incident, and in the last weeks of his life when he stayed at Auvers before committing suicide. These paintings fluctuate between tortured abstract depictions of twisted tree roots and flashes of Van Gogh at his most accomplished – _Irises,_ for example, was dashed off in a moment of inspiration between the bouts of depression that finally brought the brief life of this visionary artist to an end.

Paulus Potterstraat 7 (tel: 570 5200)
Open: Tuesday to Saturday 10am–5pm;
Sunday and public holidays 1pm–5pm
Admission charge

Trams 2, 3, 5, 12 or 16
Nearby: Rijksmuseum, Stedelijk Museum

Vincent van Gogh: Selfportrait

Scheepvaart (Maritime) Museum

*T*he Dutch Maritime Museum is housed in a massive classical building on the waterfront which was built in 1656 as the warehouse and arsenal of the Amsterdam Admiralty. Here the provisions of the Dutch navy were stored; food and fresh water, ropes and sails, cannon and cutlasses. The Admiralty employed a huge task force of cats whose job was to patrol the stores looking for rats and mice.

The sheer size and scale of the building can be judged by the fact that it now accommodates several very large historic vessels, as well as evocative paintings and maps and globes, all of which help tell the story of the Dutch maritime achievement; the story is covered exhaustively, beginning with reconstructions of ancient Roman ships and ending in the modern era of luxurious passenger liners and leisure craft.

Perhaps the most interesting part of the museum covers the Golden Age. The first Dutch expeditions to the Spice Islands – modern Indonesia – set sail in the 1590s. Their aim was to chart navigable routes to the East Indies, via the Cape of Good Hope and the Indian

The waterfront bulk of the Maritime Museum

Ocean. Reliable sea maps underpinned the rapid rise of The Netherlands as a trading nation. Among collectors of early maps, the names of Dutch cartographers such as Blau and Jansson are held in reverence for the accuracy and beauty of their work. The maps and globes displayed in the Maritime Museum are equally fascinating because they show, step by step, the charting of hitherto unexplored islands and continents such as Australia (then called New Holland), Tasmania, China, Japan and the coast of South America.

Amsterdam's shipbuilders also led the world, which is why Sir Walter Raleigh, Samuel Pepys and Tsar Peter the Great all came to the city, looking for ideas that would benefit the English and Russian navies. The museum explains the development of the sturdy three-masted merchant vessels of the 16th century which plied the oceans in search of spices and luxury goods and of the powerful warships of the Dutch fleet,

Graceful exhibits in the Maritime Museum

used to defend the nation's commercial interests whenever they were threatened.

Dutch supremacy on the seas would not have been achieved, however, without the activities of the East India Company. The first merchant voyages were financed by private entrepreneurs who, in the main, reaped a rich reward for their investment. In 1602 it was decided that Far East trade should be co-ordinated, and numerous small companies joined forces to create the East India Company. This was funded by an innovative public share flotation and the company's charter gave it almost unlimited powers. By 1669 it was synonymous with Dutch colonial power; it employed a private army and owned a huge fleet of warships and merchant vessels, having established trading outposts stretching from South Africa to the Japanese island of Deshima.

The West India Company was founded in 1621 with similar powers, to co-ordinate trade with West Africa and the Americas. It was less successful, suffering intense competition from the English, Spanish and Portuguese. One of its colonies, established on the island of Manhattan, was captured by the English in 1664, when its name was changed from New Amsterdam to New York.

The museum's account of the rise and fall of these two powerful trading companies is fascinating, but for those who find too much history indigestible there are plenty of other diversions. Children especially enjoy exploring the submarine with its periscopic views of the Amsterdam waterfront, and the reconstruction of an East Indiaman, moored in the dock outside the museum, is alone worth the price of the entrance ticket. Climbing aboard this ship you gain a very real sense of the bravery of sailors who plied the oceans in a such a vulnerable construction of wood and sailcloth; equally awesome is the vast size of the cargo hold.

Kattenburgerplein 1 (tel: 523 2222)
Open: Tuesday to Saturday, 10am–5pm,
Sunday and public holidays 1pm–5pm
(closed Monday and 1 January)
Admission charge. Buses 22 or 28
*Nearby: Docklands (see **Walk 10**),*
Kromhout Werfmuseum.

Marketplace of the World

Dutch maritime expansion in the 17th century turned Amsterdam into the world's biggest market for tropical goods. Contemporary visitors wrote of the harbour bustling with hundreds of ships so that they first glimpsed the city through a forest of masts and rigging. Timber causeways and floating wooden cranes stretched far out into the harbour. Strangers arriving after dark, when they were not allowed into the city, were lodged in one of two purpose-built floating inns.

Visitors were impressed by the sheer noise of the Beurs, the commodities exchange, where Muscovites, Persians, Turks, West Indians and traders from scores of other nations haggled over the price of sugar and spices, silks and Chinese porcelain. The city's own merchants were helped by the Bank of Amsterdam, founded in 1609, which offered loans at rates of only 3 or 4 per cent interest. With this ready source of cheap money, merchants could speculate, buying goods cheap and warehousing them until prices rose.

Warehouses remain the most visible legacy of the era. Though since turned into apartments, many retain their huge shuttered doors and pulley wheel in the gable. A maze of pipes inside carried water from rooftop cisterns for use in the event of fire – the origin of modern sprinkler systems. There are other reminders of the era in the palatial headquarters of the East India Company (see **Walk 3**) and the Schreierstoren (Tower of Tears), where sailors took leave of their wives and girlfriends before departing overseas (see **Walk 10**). Sadly, though, Amsterdam lost its maritime atmosphere in the 1880s when the old harbour was filled in to build Centraal station, thus signalling the end of the city's long and profitable relationship with the sea.

Dutch Gables

Most of the city's elegant canalside houses and warehouses were built in the 17th century. The hoists are still necessary for moving furniture since the narrow buildings only have narrow staircases.

Wall plaque

A 19th-century painting of the city's developing industrial landscape

New housing at Spaandammerburt designed by the Amsterdam School

SIX COLLECTIE
(THE SIX COLLECTION)

The Six Collection consists of a small but choice selection of 17th-century paintings displayed in the intimacy of a fine canal-side house, crammed with silver, porcelain and furniture of the age. The effect is like stepping back three centuries into the house of a wealthy merchant and art patron. The house is still a private residence – hence the need to gain a visiting card from the Rijksmuseum.

The Six family were Huguenot refugees who came to Amsterdam at the beginning of the 17th century and quickly rose to prominence. Jan Six, founder of the collection, was burgomaster, or mayor, of Amsterdam from 1691. His descendants occupied positions of influence in the city government for several generations so that the Six family is known, along with the Trips, Hoofts and Pauws, as one of the so-called 'Magnificat' families.

The Six Collection is an appropriate reflection of the family's prestige. One of the finest pictures is Rembrandt's flattering portrait of Jan Six, depicting him in reflective mood as a man of deep sensibilities and refinement. Another outstanding picture, by Frans Hals, shows Dr Tulp, a leading member of the Amsterdam Guild of Surgeons.
Amstel 218
Open: May to October, 10am–12 noon and 2pm–4pm; November to April, Monday to Friday 10am–12 noon. Entry is by means of a visiting card which can be obtained at the information desk of the Rijksmuseum. The cards are only available by booking in advance, by letter only (not in person). Visitors to the Six Collection are given a guided tour, which lasts around an hour.
Trams 4, 9 or 14
Nearby: Willet-Holthuysen Museum

SPAARNDAMMERBURT

This housing estate is one of the most characteristic examples of the work of the Amsterdam School, a group of idealistic architects who worked in the city from 1911 to 1923. Their work was stimulated by the 1901 Housing Act

The Piggy Bank Museum

which empowered the municipality to build subsidised 'council housing'. This group of architects responded with distinctive and ornamental buildings, a far cry from the box-like housing units of a later age. One of their fundamental beliefs was that the souls of the working-class occupants should be stimulated by presenting them with architecture of great aesthetic beauty.

The buildings of Spaarndammerburt make great use of deep sweeping roofs of terracotta tile, of patterned brickwork, sculpture and whimsical detail. The needle-like spire rising from the buildings on Hembrugstraat serves no purpose other than to enliven the roofscape. Straight lines are avoided in favour of gracious curving façades and window frames, giving the buildings a ship-like appearance. The architects planned every detail, down to the letter boxes and the typestyle used for house

numbering. These photogenic buildings are a joy to visit – modern, yet reminiscent of the intimate *hofjes,* or enclosed courtyards, of medieval Amsterdam.

Spaarndammerburt lies to the northwest of the Jordaan district. The best buildings are bounded by Hembrugstraat, Zaanstraat and Oostzaanstraat. Bus 22
Nearby: the Western Islands
*(see **Unknown Amsterdam**).*

SPAARPOTTENMUSEUM (PIGGY BANK MUSEUM)

Amsterdam has so many charming eccentricities that it is no surprise to find a museum devoted entirely to piggy banks and money boxes. Of the 12,000 examples in the collection, some 2,500 are on display. They range from 15th-century Javanese chests to clockwork novelties with moving figures, from precious silver and Delft to hideous plastic. Children love the toy-shop atmosphere of this entertaining museum.
Raadhuistraat 12 (tel: 556 7425)
Open: Monday to Friday 1pm–4pm
Admission charge.
Trams 13 or 17
Nearby: Koninklijk Paleis, Madame Tussaud Scenerama

Exotic skyline at Spaandammerburt

STADHUIS/MUZIEKTHEATER COMPLEX

These public buildings, on the edge of the redeveloped Jewish Quarter, are known to Amsterdammers as the Stopera complex – a contraction of Stadhuis (City Hall) and Opera, but also an ironic reference to the 'Stop the Opera' campaign of the 1970s. Controversy surrounded these buildings from the start because of the cost (300 million guilders, which activists would have preferred to see spent on housing and other social needs), the inclusion of an opera and ballet theatre (regarded as élitist) and the fact that numerous squatted houses were demolished to clear the site.

Sculpture at the Muziektheater

Despite violent protests the buildings went ahead and were completed in 1988. The controversy lingers, but in more muted form; critics regard the complex as ugly, an eyesore that is out of scale with the surrounding canal-side houses and whose bright red tile cladding clashes with their mellow brick. The Muziektheater, with its white marble cladding, is dismissively nicknamed 'the set of dentures'. It is home to The Netherlands Opera and National Ballet companies, but continues to be dogged

by poor acoustics, despite expensive attempts to remedy the problem.

Every visitor to Amsterdam should see the complex – indeed, it is hard to miss – and make up their own mind. From the inside the huge plate glass windows frame superb views and you can take advantage of free lunchtime concerts given between September and June. The arcade linking the two parts of the complex has a mural showing a cross-section through The Netherlands to illustrate Normaal Amsterdams Peil – Normal Amsterdam Level – the standard ordnance datum by which heights are measured in this country where half the land lies below sea level.

Waterlooplein (tel: 552 9111 administration; 625 5455 box office) Open: Monday to Saturday 10am–6pm, Sunday 12 noon–6pm. Guided tours Wednesday and Saturday 4pm Admission free but there is a charge for guided tours Trams 9 or 14 Nearby: Waterlooplein Flea Market (see Markets), Rembrandthuis

STEDELIJK MUSEUM

From the outside, the Stedelijk Museum (Museum of Modern Art) gives no clue to its contents. The turreted neo-Renaissance building, dating from 1895, once housed a collection of antiques given by the Dowager of Jonkheer. If the Dowager were to return she would be shocked: her collection has gone, the walls have all been painted white to mask the ornamental detail and the walls are hung with bold and uncompromisingly modern works of art.

The main drawback of the museum is that you never know what will be on display. Despite its palatial dimensions, the building is too small to show the

At the Stedelijk Museum

entire art collection, which spans the period 1850 to the present day. Instead, selections are made to illustrate the development of a particular artist or movement.

This approach is exemplified by one of the permanent exhibits, a room devoted to the work of the Russian artist, Kasimir Malevitch. The works were chosen by the artist himself and the accompanying text explains his personal evolution from realism, through Cubism to 'suprematism', a form of art that is concerned with the essence of colour, form and technique rather than representation. The display seems aimed at sceptical visitors who may not be aware that abstraction is a conscious artistic choice, not a reflection on the artist's ability, or inability, to draw.

The rest of the material on display comes without interpretive labelling – after all, it is a fundamental tenet of modern art movements that art is about itself and cannot be reduced, or

paraphrased, by verbal statements. Thus visitors wander through rooms hung with the familiar – paintings by Cézanne, Chagall, Mondrian and Picasso – and the puzzling – Barnett Newman's vast monochrome canvases and Keinholz's _The Beanery,_ a three-dimensional reconstruction of a seedy Los Angeles bar where all the drinkers have clocks for faces.

Having wrestled, mentally, with works that range from the stimulating to the sterile, it is a relief to know that the downstairs café/restaurant, overlooking the sculpture garden, serves some of the best salad lunches in Amsterdam.

Paulus Potterstraat 13 (tel: 573 2911)
Open: daily 11am–5pm; public holidays
11am–4pm (closed 1 January)
Admission charge
Trams 2, 3, 5, 12, 15 or 16
Nearby: Rijksmuseum, Rijksmuseum
Vincent Van Gogh

'Art is about itself'

TECHNOLOGIE MUSEUM NINT

Amsterdam's science and technology museum is located in the former Asscher diamond-cutting factory, now the Dutch Institute for Industry and Technology. The museum is full of push-button models that explain modern developments in science – telephones, computers, holograms, automobiles, bar-code readers and computer-aided design techniques. It is questionable how much of the underlying theory is absorbed by the numerous children who fill this friendly museum, but it is undeniably fun and takes the seriousness out of science. There are plans in hand

The flamboyant façade of the Theater Instituut

to create an even bigger Science Centre by 1993 (check with the VVV Tourist Information Centre for details).
Tolstraat 129 (tel: 675 4211)
Open: Monday to Friday 10am–5pm;
Saturday, Sunday and public holidays 12
noon–5pm (closed 1 January, 30 April and
25 December)
Admission charge
Tram 4

THEATER INSTITUUT

The Nederlands Theatre Institute is housed in a splendid 17th-century building, which is worth seeing in its own right. The house was purchased in 1638 by Michael Pauw, founder of the Dutch West India Company, and transformed by the leading Golden Age architect, Philips Vingboons. For the façade, Vingboons designed the first ever 'neck gable', so called because of its resemblance to the neck and shoulders of a wine bottle. The device was to prove popular and was widely copied by other Amsterdam architects.

The murals and ceiling paintings of the interior, depicting landscapes and biblical subjects, date from a refurbishment in 1728 and are the work of the leading artists of their day, Jacob de Wit and Isaac de Moucheron. These are complemented by lavish stucco work and a magnificent spiral staircase.

The museum itself tells the story of Dutch theatre from the 17th century up to the modern age of TV, film and video, through a range of fascinating exhibits. These include a miniature theatre dating from 1781, a fine costume collection, props, models illustrating the backstage work of scenery, lighting and stage effects, even a wind and rain machine. There is also a garden where tea is served, a popular meeting place for

actors, writers and directors.
Herengracht 168 (tel: 623 5104)
Open: Tuesday to Sunday and public
holidays 11am–5pm (closed Monday, 25
December, 1 January and 30 April)
Admission charge
Trams 13, 14, 17 or bus 21
Nearby: Spaarpottenmuseum.

TROPENMUSEUM (TROPICAL MUSEUM)

The Tropical Museum is housed in the former Dutch Colonial Institute, a whimsical building of minaret-like towers, designed in the 'eclectic' style and completed in 1923. The façades are decorated with reliefs depicting the peoples of the East, the cultivation of the most important crops of the former colonies – rubber, tobacco, sugar and rice – and four of the major world religions, animism, Hinduism, Islam and Christianity.

The museum was transformed in the 1970s from a celebration of Dutch imperialism to something altogether more exciting. The museum now illustrates life in India, Southeast Asia and South America through colourful and authentic reconstructions of huts, houses, bazaars and shops, complete with characteristic smells; only the heat and flies are missing and background tapes play continuously to evoke the noise and bustle of the streets.

Visitors wander in and out of the displays making their own discoveries and it is easy to lose yourself for hours, especially if you settle down to watch some of the documentary video tapes dealing with Third World problems, such as rainforest depletion and population growth. The museum also hosts numerous cultural events, from Indonesian gamelan concerts (September to June, first Sunday in each month at 3pm) to modern African dance and music.
Linnaeusstraat 2 (tel: 568 8295)
Open: Monday to Friday 10am–5pm;
Saturday, Sunday and public holidays
12 noon–5pm (closed 1 January, 30 April,
5 May and 25 December)
Admission charge
Trams 9, 10, 14 or bus 22
Nearby: Kindermuseum TM Junior

The world explored at the Tropical Museum

Ethnic Amsterdam

Nearly a quarter of Amsterdam's population is of non-Dutch origin, a legacy of colonialism and of the 'guest workers' policy of the 1960s. Before World War II the Dutch Empire spanned the globe, from the Antilles and Dutch Guyana to South Africa, and from there, via the 8,000 islands of the East Indies, to Tasmania. In 1949 Indonesia was the first of the former colonies to secure independence, but ties between the two countries remain strong; thousands of Amsterdammers have island ancestry and their contribution to city life is most evident in the large number of excellent Indonesian restaurants.

Dutch Guyana – modern Surinam – gained independence as recently as 1975 and 150,000 Surinamese have since exercised their right to settle in The Netherlands. Another 35,000 migrants from Turkey and Morocco arrived in the 1960s, deliberately imported to do the low-paid manual jobs that the Dutch themselves were not willing to do.

Amsterdammers pride themselves on a long tradition of hospitality, but tension nevertheless exists between different parts of the community. Some white residents blame incomers for crime and complain about the cost to the city of housing, welfare and unemployment benefits. Equally, immigrants blame crime on the white population, whom they see as immoral and irreligious, and they complain that their cultures are misunderstood.

Even so, great efforts are being made to create a harmonious society. The area known as De Pijp (The Pipe) is a good example of successful integration. Most residents here are young and determined to get on. Albert Cuypstraat, the area's colourful market, is a cheerful melting pot, an exotic bazaar catering to all tastes, and the best place to experience Amsterdam in all its ethnic diversity.

Unknown Amsterdam: the Western Islands

*I*f you have fallen in love with Amsterdam and want to buy a bijou city residence, you could do worse than head for the three man-made islands located in the western harbour. Prinseneiland, Reileneiland and Bickerseiland – collectively the Westerlijk (Western) Eilands – were constructed in the 1630s, originally for the storage of hazardous and inflammable materials well away from the residential heart of the city. The stately 17th-century warehouses survive, with their huge sail-shaped window shutters. Some have already been turned into apartments, while others are in the process of being converted. Some are still used for their original purpose, storing tropical imports such as timber. Unconverted warehouses are much in demand by artists, sculptors and photographers because of their huge floor area and bohemian ambience.

As a result the Western Islands have a distinctive 'village' atmosphere, enhanced by the lack of traffic. Herons perch on the ancient lifting bridges that link the islands, all as attractive and as well preserved as the more famous Magerebrug in the city centre. Swans, moorhens and ducks nest on the canal banks where expensive yachts are moored alongside tugs, barges and

A wealth of gables to be enjoyed at Zandhoek

wrecked hulls – their owners intending, optimistically, to restore them...one day.

The best way to reach the islands from Amsterdam Centraal station is to walk down Haarlemmerstraat and Haarlemmerdijk, the latter a characterful street lined by inexpensive neighbourhood shops and cafés; this is the 'real' Amsterdam, untouched by tourism, where ordinary residents shop and pass the time of day. The street ends at Haarlemmerplein where a ponderous triumphal arch, built in the 19th century as a monumental entrance to the city from Haarlem, now stands unloved in the middle of a busy traffic island.

Turn right, crossing the busy road, then pass under the railway viaduct. Suddenly you are in a different world. Take the first bridge on the right and you will reach Prinseneiland where the best apartments are located. Continue straight through and you will hear the sounds of hens and goats as you turn left on Bickersgracht; the source is the Kinderboerderij Om de Hoek, the

Children's Farm on the Corner, just up around the bend (open daylight hours, free admission but donations welcome).

Carry on and you will reach Zandhoek where there is a fine row of 17th-century houses with spout, step and bell gables. Plaques on the house fronts depict Noah's Ark, St Peter and St John, anchors, boats and a white horse. The last in the row, no 15, is a friendly restaurant, De Gouden Raeal, renowned for its inexpensive regional French cuisine.

Beyond this point the scene becomes more bleak. A couple of warehouses on Van Diemenstraat have been turned into nightclubs, including no 8 – Joseph Lam's Dixieland Jazz Club – which is packed every weekend, despite its unpromising location. Otherwise the empty warehouses are waiting for the IJ-Oever project to commence, a hugely ambitious regeneration plan designed to provide yet more conference centres, marinas, parks and museums as well as homes for 20,000 families and office premises designed to attract multi-national companies.

Walk all the way back to Bickerstraat until you reach Zeilmakerstraat on the left. Here, at no 15, you will find the Amsterdams Beeldhouwers Kollektief (the Sculptors' Collective), just the place to buy a small bronze for the house or a marble statue for the garden (open Wednesday to Friday, 10am–5pm; Saturday and Sunday 12 noon–5pm). Dutch buyers are more fortunate than foreign visitors – they can take out an interest-free loan from the government to buy the works on display, repaying in instalments. The idea is to encourage people of ordinary means to buy art.

Continue and, all too soon, you will emerge beneath the railway viaduct

Sculpture at the Sculptors' Collective

again; cross the road, walk straight on and you will find yourself back in Haarlemmerdijk.

VAN LOON, MUSEUM

The atmospheric Museum Van Loon
was designed in 1672 by Adriaan
Dortsman and has the figures of
Minerva, Mars, Vulcan and Ceres on the
cornice. One of the first owners of the
house was Ferdinand Bol, a pupil of
Rembrandt, who married a rich wife and
promptly gave up painting. Another was
Catharina Trip whose initials, along with
those of her husband, Abraham van
Hagen, are carved into the staircase
balustrade. The house was purchased in
1884 by Hendrik van Loon and it now
features a near-complete sequence of van
Loon family portraits, from 17th-century
paintings to 20th-century photographs.
The period furnishings all have the
patina that comes from time and use,
creating a mood of faded grandeur.
Keizersgracht 672 (tel: 624 5255)
Open: Monday 10am–5pm;
Sunday 1pm–5pm
Admission charge
Trams 16, 24 or 25
Nearby: Museum Fodor

The glowing interior of the Museum
Van Loon

VERZETSMUSEUM (DUTCH RESISTANCE MUSEUM)

The Dutch Resistance Museum is
housed in a former synagogue in the
wealthy Amsterdam South suburb where
Anne Frank and her family lived until
they went into hiding. The displays
recall the many ingenious ways that the
Dutch Resistance sought to sabotage the
Nazi occupation. The exhibits include a
bicycle-powered printing press used for
forging documents to help Jews escape
arrest and for producing underground
newspapers – such as *Het Parool* (The
Password), which continues to circulate
in Amsterdam to this day.

There is a reconstruction of a hiding
place used by *onderduikers,* 'divers', along
with contemporary photographs, video
material and radio broadcasts all of
which help to bring this fascinating
subject vividly to life.
Lekstraat 63 (tel: 644 9797)
Open: Tuesday to Friday 10am–5pm;
Saturday, Sunday and public holidays
1pm–5pm (closed Monday, 1 January,
4 May and 25 December)
Admission charge
Trams 4 or 25

WILLET-HOLTHUYSEN, MUSEUM

Of the several Golden Age houses open
to the public in Amsterdam, this is the
grandest. The imposing mansion was
built in 1689 and left to the city in 1895
along with a large collection of glass,
Delftware, clocks, furniture and silver.
At first nobody wanted to see a house
full of 'Victorian' furniture little different
to that which many Amsterdammers had
in their own home. The bored curator
spent his time writing a scurrilous novel
about the former owners and it was
jokingly said that the museum was an

The Willet-Holthuysen Museum

ideal place for clandestine lovers to meet without being observed. Visitors now come in considerable numbers, entering through the tradesman's door beneath the steps for a glimpse of the 18th-century kitchen, stacked with gleaming copper pans. Next comes an audio-visual presentation on the house as a prelude to the grander rooms upstairs, with their ceiling paintings, Aubusson tapestries and gilded chandeliers.
Herengracht 605 (tel: 523 1870)
Open: daily 11am–5pm (closed 1 January)
Admission charge
Trams 4, 9 or 14
Nearby: Six Collection

ZOO (ARTIS)

Amsterdam's zoo opened in 1838 under the grand title of Natura Artis Magistra (Nature, Teacher of the Arts). Now known simply as Artis, the zoo offers enough attractions to fill the best part of a day. As well as 6,000 animals kept in naturalistic enclosures, there is a children's farm, a spectacular planetarium, a tropical house and a large aquarium. The ticket includes admission to two museums on the site – the Geologisch Museum illustrating the earth's evolution and the Zoologisch Museum whose tableaux and audio-visuals explain the flora and fauna of characteristic Dutch landscapes.
Plantage Kerklaan 40 (tel: 523 3400)
Open: daily 9am–5pm
(planetarium closed Monday until 1pm;
Zoologisch Museum closed Monday)
Admission charge
Trams 7, 9 or 14
Nearby: Hortus Botanicus

Getting to know you at Amsterdam zoo

Amsterdam Environs

INTRODUCTION

Travel within The Netherlands is
extremely easy thanks to an excellent
integrated public transport system.
Many of the sites covered in this section
are accessible by fast, cheap and reliable
intercity trains which depart from
Amsterdam Centraal station every 15 or
30 minutes. Journey times are short –
Haarlem is only 13 minutes away,
Utrecht 28 minutes, Den Haag (The
Hague) 35 minutes and Rotterdam an
hour. Amsterdam therefore makes a
perfect base for exploring the wider

Harbour view of Rotterdam

centre in Amsterdam Centraal station or
by ringing 620 2266 (international) or
06 899 1121 (national).

Some destinations close to
Amsterdam are not on the rail network
but are easily reached by buses that go
from the main terminus outside
Amsterdam Centraal station, or from the
suburban station, Amsterdam Amstel. If
you prefer to have everything organised
for you, there are numerous coach tours

A sunny street in Volendam

attractions of The Netherlands. All-
inclusive day-trip tickets offer the
cheapest way to travel; they include the
cost of the rail fare, bus links, admission
fees and refreshments, all at a discount.
Over 50 destinations are covered by this
scheme.

Alternatively you can buy a one-day
Rail Rover ticket which allows unlimited
use of the transport network. Details of
both are given in the *Holland by Train*
leaflet available from the information

The bridge at Haarlem

covering the same destinations. These can be booked at the VVV Informatiekantoor (tourist information centre) on Stationsplein in Amsterdam *(tel: 020 626 6444)* or through offices of Thomas Cook.

Once you arrive at your destination you can obtain free maps and leaflets from the excellent VVV tourist information centres which are usually located on the main square or near the station. You can also hire a bike for the day at most stations by presenting your ticket and paying a small deposit.

There is much to see and do within a short distance of Amsterdam.

AMSTERDAM-ENVIRONS

0 10 20 30 40 km
0   10   20 miles

Harlingen · Franeker · **Leeuwarden**
Waddenzee · Drachten
Den Burg · Bolsward
Texel · Sneek
Den Helder · Den Oever · *Fluessen*
· *Gaasterland* Heerenveen
Anna Paulowna · *Tjeuke Meer*
Schagen · *IJsselmeer* Lemmer
· Medemblik · *Noordoost* Steenwijk
Heerhugowaard · Enkhuizen · *polder*
Bergen · Urk · Vollenhove · Meppel
Alkmaar · Hoorn
Heiloo · *Markermeer* · Ketelmeer · Kampen
Castricum · *Flevoland*
Beverwijk · Purmerend · Edam · Lelystad
Ijmuiden · Zaandijk · Volendam · **Zwolle**
Zaandam · *Marken* · Monnickendam
Haarlem · **AMSTERDAM**
Zandvoort · Almere · Heerde · *IJssel*
Heemstede · Muiden · Harderwijk
Keukenhof Schiphol · Ouderkerk · Naarden · Epe · Olst
· Lisse · Aalsmeer · Abcoude · Bussum · Ermelo · **Schloss Het Loo** **Deventer**
Katwijk aan Zee · **Hilversum** · Nijkerk · **Apeldoorn**
Vogelpark · Breukelen · **Palais Soestdijk**
Wassenaar · **Leiden** · **Amersfoort**
Scheveningen · **Tierpark** Alphen a/d Rijn · **Schloss De Haar** Soest · Barneveld · Zutphen
Den Haag · Boskoop · Woerden **Utrecht**
Hoek van · Zeist · Ede **National Park de Hoge Veluwe**
Holland · Doorn
Delft · Berkel · Ijsselstein · Veenendaal · *Neder-* **Arnhem**
Europoort · Gouda · *Lek* · Wageningen · *Rijn* Zevenaar
Vlaardingen · **Rotterdam** · *Amsterdam-Rijn-kanaal*
· Alblasserdam · Leerdam · Tiel · **Nijmegen**
Haringvliet · *Maas* · Gorinchem · *Waal* · *Maas* · Wijchen
Overflakkee · **Dordrecht**
· *Hollands Diep* · Oss · Grave
· Made · Waalwijk · **'s-Hertogenbosch**

D

AALSMEER

The Aalsmeer Flower Auction (Verenigde Bloemenveilingen Aalsmeer, or VBA) is the biggest commercial flower market in the world. It is well worth visiting if you are fond of plants or just enjoy the bustle of a busy commercial market. You do have to be an early riser, however, since most of the action takes place between 7.30am and 11.00am (closed Saturday, Sunday and holidays).

Visitors watch the proceedings from an elevated gallery which provides a bird's-eye view of the auction itself and all the sorting and despatch work that goes on behind the scenes. Recorded commentaries, in seven languages, explain what is going on.

The VBA, founded in 1968, is a co-operative venture with a membership of 5,000 growers who sell their pot plants and cut plants at Aalsmeer, paying a commission of 5 per cent of sales to fund the operation.

Sales are conducted using the 'Dutch auction' system. This works in the opposite way to normal auction procedure, with prices starting at the top and coming down until a buyer is found. Prices are indicated by a huge clock above the auctioneer's head marked out in divisions from 100 down to 1. The

The distinctive national dress

clock pointer starts at 100 – the highest price – and sweeps downwards until a buyer, seated at a computerised desk, presses a button to stop the clock at the price he or she is prepared to pay. Computerisation is the key to the speed and efficiency of the whole operation. Invoices and despatch information are prepared automatically as soon as the 'buy' button is pressed. The computer also handles all the currency calculations – more than 80 per cent of the produce sold here is exported.

Some 10,000 transactions an hour are conducted in this way in five separate auction rooms devoted to different types of plant. The lots are delivered to the buyer within 15 minutes of the sale; around 350 buyers rent packing space on the premises and some 2,000 trucks, laden with sweet-smelling produce, leave the building daily for all parts of Europe.

The market is huge; with an area equivalent to 100 football pitches (30 hectares) it is said to be the biggest commercial building in the world.

An auction of colour at Aalsmeer

Market staff use bicycles to get around. Aalsmeer is big business in every way; The Netherlands is the world's leading producer of pot plants and flowers, with 51 per cent of the market, and much of that produce passes here.

On the lighter side, everyone involved in the market – growers, buyers and florists – stages a huge and colourful parade from Aalsmeer to the centre of Amsterdam annually on the first Sunday in September, consisting of imaginatively decorated cars and trucks smothered beneath a massive tapestry of flowers.

Location: 12km southwest of Amsterdam at Legmeerdijk 313, Aalsmeer

Getting there: Bus 172 from Amsterdam Centraal station (tel: 02977 34567/32185)

Open: April to September, Monday to Friday 7.30am–12 noon.

ALKMAAR

Alkmaar is famed for the traditional cheese market held in the main square every Friday morning in summer months. White-garbed porters in straw hats (red, green, blue or yellow denoting the particular group to which they belong) carry the huge rounds of yellow-waxed cheese on wooden sledges across the square into the Renaissance **Waaggebouw** (Weigh House) where the actual selling takes place. The streets around the square are crammed with stalls selling antiques, crafts and – of course – local cheese. Barrel organs and buskers add to the festive atmosphere. The town itself has several fine buildings: the 15th-century **Grote Kerk** (Great Church), the **Stadhuis** (Town Hall) of 1520 and the Waaggebouw of 1582 (housing a cheese museum) can all be visited, and the **Stedelijk Museum** has an interesting collection of antique toys.

Location: 37km northwest of Amsterdam

Getting there: train line 1 (to Den Helder); journey time 32 minutes

Tourist information: Waagplein 3 (tel: 072 114 284)

Open: Cheese market mid-April to mid-September, Friday 10am–12 noon.

Say cheese at Aalkmaar

ARNHEM

The name of Arnhem will always be associated with Operation Market Garden, the heroic but disastrous World War II battle which was immortalised in the film, *A Bridge Too Far*. The battle was an ambitious attempt to end the war in time for Christmas 1944. The military leaders involved, Field Marshal Montgomery and General Eisenhower, planned to invade Germany after capturing the strategic Rhine bridge at Arnhem. This involved flying troops into the heart of The Netherlands, still under Nazi occupation. General Browning, in charge of the Airborne Divisions, had misgivings about the operation and it was he who told Montgomery; 'We might be going a bridge too far'. He was right; when 35,000 troops were parachuted into Arnhem on 17 September 1944 they found the bridges heavily defended by the tanks and artillery of the 2nd SS Panzer Division. Some 600 Allied troops fought their way

A windmill at the Arnhem Folk Museum

to Arnhem bridge and defended it for four days before being forced to withdraw. The battle ended with defeat for the Allies and the death of thousands of soldiers.

Visitors can visit the battle sites and trace the course of events, by means of models and an audio-visual presentation, at the **Airborne Museum** in Oosterbeek, 8km west of Arnhem. Nearby, on the north bank of the Rhine, is the **Oosterbeek War Cemetery**, beautifully maintained by the War Graves Commission.

Arnhem has two other outstanding attractions. On the outskirts of the town is the **Nederlands Openlucht (Open-Air) Museum** where 100 traditional buildings have been rescued from their original sites and reconstructed. They include windmills, farmhouses, schools, churches and inns dating back to the 17th century. The interiors are used to display traditional costumes, folk art, furniture and tools and the museum regularly mounts craft demonstrations.

Some 6km to the north of Arnhem is the Hoge Veluwe National Park, a huge tract of forest and heath. Free bikes provide the means of getting around and the main highlight is the Kröller Müller Museum, at the centre of the park, where over 200 works by Van Gogh are displayed together with works by Picasso, Braque and many modern artists. In the sculpture park around the museum, works by Henry Moore, Rodin, Barbara Hepworth and others are all the more entrancing for their background of trees, water and open skies.

Location: 72km southeast of Amsterdam
Getting there: train lines 4 and 5
(to Nijmegen); journey time 75 minutes;
change at Arnhem for Oosterbeek, journey
time 4 minutes. Bus 3 (to Alteveer) goes
from Arnhem station to the Openlucht
Museum and bus 107 (to Lelystad) goes to
the Hoge Veluwe Park; in summer a special
museum bus, No 12, serves both museums
Tourist information: Stationsplein 45
(tel: 085 420 330)
Open: Airborne Museum Monday to
Saturday 11am–5pm, Sunday and public
holidays 12 noon–5pm; Openlucht Museum
April to October daily 9am–5pm; Hoge
Veluwe Park daily 8am–sunset; Kröller
Müller Museum Tuesday to Saturday
10am–5pm, Sunday and public holidays
11am–5pm.

AVIODOME (NETHERLANDS NATIONAL AEROSPACE MUSEUM)

This is a museum to visit when killing time at the airport, since it is only a short walk away from the terminal. It is also popular with children, who are allowed to climb into the cockpit of one of the aircraft. The dome-shaped building shelters various historic aircraft, ranging from the Wright Flyer of 1903 to a Mercury space capsule. It also celebrates the Dutch contribution to aviation history; the Dutch national carrier, KLM, was the world's first commercial airline, flying locally built Fokker FVII aircraft from 1919. Posters and KLM memorabilia of the 1920s evoke the romance of flight in those early days. There is a sober reminder of the aerial warfare of World War II in the salvaged remains of a British bomber, and plenty of diversions in the form of films, slide shows and an exhibition on the importance of Schiphol airport to the Dutch economy.

Location: Westelijke Randweg Schiphol
Centrum, Schiphol Airport (tel: 604 1521)
Getting there: train to Schiphol station then
follow the signs; 10 minutes walk
Open: May to September, daily 10am–
5pm; October to 1 May, Monday to Friday
10am–5pm, Saturday and Sunday
12 noon–5pm (closed 4 May, 25, 31
December and 1 January)
Admission charge

The Schiphol Aviodome is popular with visitors of all ages

DELFT

Delft has given its name to the distinctive blue and white pottery that has been produced here since the 17th century when East India Company ships first started bringing back delicate porcelain wares from China. The potters of the region immediately began to copy these wares but decorated their plates, jugs, tiles and tulip jars with scenes from everyday life, biblical subjects and Dutch landscapes. The industry nearly collapsed in the 19th century in the face of competition from England. The only firm to survive in Delft was De Porceleyne Fles, founded in 1653 and

The lovely Prinsenhof Museum at Delft

still going strong. If you want to know more you should head straight for this company's Visitor Centre which exhibits typical products and offers factory tours throughout the day.

There is, though, far more to Delft than pottery. On the main square, Markt, you will find the Renaissance Stadhuis (Town Hall) built in 1618 by Hendrik de Keyser. The statue in the centre of the square commemorates the lawyer Hugo Grotius, born in Delft in 1583, whose great work on the conduct of war laid the foundations for modern international law.

Opposite, Nieuwe Kerk, with its soaring 15th-century choir, contains the mausoleum of William the Silent, leader of the Dutch revolt against Spanish rule and the father of The Netherlands. The monument, another work by Hendrik de Keyser, was designed in 1614; in allegorical form, it depicts the ideals on which the newly independent Dutch Republic was based – liberty, justice, religion and fortitude.

William the Silent met an untimely end in Delft in 1584; he was assassinated in the nearby convent of St Agatha, now the **Prinsenhof Museum** which William used as his campaign headquarters during the war against Spain. The bullet holes made by his assassin (Balthazar Gerards, a fanatical Catholic and a supporter of Spanish rule) can be seen behind glass in room 8, the Moordzaal (Death Hall).

Apart from this morbid memorial, the rest of the museum is a delight. The traceried Gothic windows of the 15th-century convent look out on to attractive courtyard gardens and the walls are hung with paintings by artists of the Delft School.

Opposite the museum is the 14th-century **Oude Kerk**, with its leaning tower and beautiful 16th-century transept, built in the style known, appropriately, as Flamboyant Gothic. Inside there are the tombs of Vermeer and the Delft-born inventor of the microscope, Antonie van Leeuwenhoek, along with memorials to the Admirals Piet Hein and Maarten Tromp; the latter's tomb is carved with a realistic battle scene praised by Samuel Pepys as 'a sea-fight cut in marble, the smoke the

Tempting displays in Delft

best expressed that ever I saw'.

From the church it is worth walking the length of Oude Delft, a leafy canal lined by elegant houses. At no 199 the best collection of antique Delftware in the city can be found, housed in the **Huis Lambert van Meerten Museum**; the interior is covered in tiles, ranging from large-scale battle scenes to cheerful depictions of children's games.

At the opposite end of Oude Delft, the courtyard houses at no 39 once served as an office of the VOC (Verenigde Oostindische Companie – better known as the East India Company). Opposite the huge former arsenal, the Armamentarium, is now the **Nederlands Legermuseum** (Dutch Army Museum).

Location: 58km southwest of Amsterdam
Getting there: train line 3 to Den Haag (The Hague), then change to line 2; journey time 40 minutes
Tourist information: Markt 85 (tel: 015 126 100)

DELFT

De Porceleyene Fles
Rotterdamseweg 196 (tel: 015 569 214). Open: Monday to Saturday 9am–5pm. Admission free

Huis Lambert van Meerten Museum
Oude Delft 199 (tel: 015 121 858). Open: Tuesday to Saturday 10am–6pm, Sunday 1pm–5pm. Admission charge

Nederlands Legermuseum
Korte Geer. Open: Tuesday to Saturday 10am–5pm, Sunday 1pm– 5pm. Admission charge

Nieuwe Kerk
Markt. Open: April to October, Monday to Saturday 9am–5pm; November to May, Monday to Friday 10am–12 noon and 1.30pm– 4pm. Admission charge

Oude Kerk
Oude Delft. Open: April to October, Monday to Saturday 12 noon–4pm. Admission charge

Prinsenhof Museum
St Agathaplein 1 (tel: 015 602 357). Open: Tuesday to Saturday 10am– 5pm, Sunday 1pm–5pm. Admission charge

EDAM

Edam competes with Gouda for the title of cheese capital of The Netherlands; in terms of sheer quantity of output Edam wins but, in contrast to Gouda, Edam has not turned its cheese industry into a major tourist attraction. Instead the town is noted for the quiet calm of its numerous waterways and wooden bridges, though visitors can buy the familiar round balls of soft cheese, wrapped in a protective skin of red wax, at the ancient **Kaasmarkt** (Cheese Market) on Waagplein, built in 1592.

The delightful **Edams Museum** on Damplein occupies a late Gothic house

Serenity and cheese at Edam

of 1530 whose small dark rooms, ladder-like stairs and hidden cupboard beds are reminiscent of life on board a ship. The building even has a curious floating cellar which sways as you walk across the floor – built, according to the local story, by a retired ship's captain who was nostalgic for the feel of the sea. Equally eccentric are the museum's portraits of three local characters, one extremely fat, another very tall and the third, Pieter Langebaard, who had, true to his name, a very long beard; he toured The Netherlands showing it off in order to raise funds for the local orphanage.

The town's other important monument is the **Grote Kerk** (Great Church) rebuilt after a fire in 1602 and notable for its stained glass of 1606 depicting trademarks and historical scenes. Several operators offer boat tours in summer from Edam to neighbouring towns around the shore of the former Zuider Zee.

Location: 22km north of Amsterdam
Getting there: Bus 114 from Amsterdam Centraal station; journey time 35 minutes
Tourist information: Kleine Kerkstraat 17 (tel: 02993 71727)
Open: Kaasmarkt, April to September, daily 10am–5pm; Edams Museum, April to September, Monday to Saturday 10am–4.30pm, Sunday 2pm–4.30pm.

GOUDA

For those interested in the traditional cheese market, Gouda should be visited on Thursday mornings in summer. Here white-coated experts handle and sample the cheese with all the respect usually reserved for the finest wines. Gouda develops different characteristics as it ages and several types are sold: *jong* (young) is creamy and mild, *belegen* is firmer and has matured for four months, *oud* (old) is 10 months old and *overjarig,* the most expensive, is at least a year old and should be pungent and crumbly. In addition there are cumin *(komijn)* and clove *(nagel)* flavoured varieties.

The market takes place against the backdrop of the fine Flemish-style **Stadhuis**, built in 1450 and decorated with statues of Burgundian counts and countesses, a reminder that this part of The Netherlands was under Burgundian rule in the 15th century.

The medieval quarter, with its quiet cobbled lanes, lies to the south of the Markt. **St Janskerk** has the best stained glass in The Netherlands, a magnificent series of windows given by various donors when the church was rebuilt after a fire in 1522. Local guilds were among the sponsors and they chose appropriate biblical themes – *Jonah and the Whale* for the fishmongers, *Balaam and his Ass* for the butchers. Philip II of Spain donated *The Last Supper* and he is depicted with his wife, Queen Mary I of England. William the Silent, who was shortly to lead the Dutch revolt against Philip II's rule, donated *Christ Driving the Money Changers from the Temple.*

Opposite the church is the **Catharina Gasthuis**, founded as a hospice for travellers in the 14th century, now housing a fine collection of medieval art and Impressionist paintings by members of The Hague School. The town's other museum, **De Moriaan** (The Moor) is a beautifully preserved 17th-century tobacco shop displaying a collection of clay pipes, located on the former harbour at Westhaven 29.
Location: 52km south of Amsterdam
Getting there: train line 5 or 7 to Utrecht then change for line 4, 8, or 11; journey time 50 minutes

The stained-glass window at Gouda is part of a series of windows at St Janskerk, each of which tells a story in jewel-like colours

Tourist information: Markt 27
(tel: 01820 13666)
Open: Cheese market, June to August Thursday 9am–12 noon; St Janskerk, April to October, Monday to Saturday 9am–5pm, November to March, Monday to Saturday 10am–4pm; Catharina Gasthuis, Monday to Saturday 10am–5pm, Sunday 12 noon–5pm; De Moriaan, Monday to Friday 10am–5pm, Saturday 10am–12.30pm and 1.30pm–5pm, Sunday 12 noon–5pm.

DEN HAAG (THE HAGUE)

After Amsterdam, Den Haag has more to offer than any other city in The Netherlands and the museums alone will occupy more than a day, so it is worth considering an overnight stay. Den Haag is an abbreviated form of the city's old name, 's Gravenhaage, meaning the Count's Hedge. This hedge surrounded the hunting lodge of the medieval Counts of Holland, later rebuilt as a castle. The town grew up around the castle and its future was assured when Den Haag became the political capital of The Netherlands in 1586, chosen because it offered a neutral meeting ground for the leaders of the seven independent provinces created under the Treaty of Utrecht after the Spanish had been driven out.

The former castle of the Counts of Holland, the 13th-century Ridderzaal, still stands at the heart of the city. It is surrounded by the buildings of the Dutch Parliament on one side and by the Mauritshuis Museum on the other, a graceful building whose façade is reflected in the Hof Vijver lake, all that remains of the original castle moat. The Mauritshuis contains several important works: Rogier van de Weyden's *Lamentation,* Rembrandt's *The Anatomy Lesson of Dr Tulp,* his first public commission, the charming *Goldfinch,* by Rembrandt's gifted pupil, Fabritius, and Vermeer's *View of Delft.* Andy Warhol's *Queen Beatrix* brings the collection up to date.

The Mauritshuis is only one of several museums surrounding Hof Vijver; within a short stroll you can sample the popular Gavengenpoort, once a prison and now a 'torture museum', or the Schilderijengalerie Willem V (Buitenhof 35), a small gallery crammed with Old Masters. The Haags Historisch Museum (Korte Vijverberg 7) displays old paintings of the city.

If shopping appeals more than museums, head for The Passage, off Buitenhof, an elegant 19th-century arcade. This leads to the pedestrianised shopping streets around the 15th-century Oudekerk. Noordeindestraat is definitely for the wealthy with its couturiers, art and antique dealers and up-market restaurants patronised by local diplomats.

Continuing up this street, past the royal Paleis Noordeinde, you will reach the Panorama Mesdag, an intriguing relic of the 19th century and a fine example of *trompe l'oeil* painting. The circular canvas, 120m long, shows an extraordinarily realistic view of the nearby coastal resort of Scheveningen as it was in 1881. More works by Hendrik Mesdag, a leading Impressionist painter of The Hague School, can be seen at the artist's former home, now the Museum Mesdag, nearby at Laan van Meerdevoort 7. Just to the north is the huge Vredespaleis (Peace Palace) founded after The Hague Peace Conference of 1899 and financed by the Scottish millionaire Andrew Carnegie. The aim was to provide a forum for resolving international disputes - a worthy aim though it did not prevent two world wars. Now it is the seat of the International Court of Justice.

Beyond this point there awaits the best of the city's museums, the Haags Gemeentemuseum. This has a big collection of modern art, from The Hague School to Mondrian, of Delftware, musical instruments and of historic costume. The Omniversum planetarium next door appeals to

Gavengenpoort
*Buitenhof 30. Open: April to September,
Monday to Friday 10am– 5pm,
Saturday and Sunday 1pm–5pm.
Admission charge*
Haags Gemeentenmuseum
*Stadhouderslaan 41 (tel: 070 351
4181). Open: Tuesday to Friday
10am–5pm, Saturday and Sunday
1pm–5pm. Admission charge*
Madurodam
*Haringkade 175 (tel: 070 355 3900).
Open: mid-March to June daily 9am–
10pm; June to August daily 9am–11pm;
September daily 9am–9.30pm; October
to December daily 9am–6pm.
Admission charge*
Mauritshuis Museum
*Plein 29 (tel: 070 346 9244). Open:
Tuesday to Saturday 10am–5pm,
Sunday 11am–5pm.
Admission charge*
Omniversum
*President Kennedylaan 5 (tel: 070 354
5454). Open: Tuesday to Thursday
11am–4pm, Friday to Sunday
11am–9pm; planetarium performances
on the hour. Admission charge*
Panorama Mesdag
*Zeestraat 65B (tel: 070 364 2563).
Open: Monday to Saturday 10am–
5pm, Sunday 12 noon–5pm. Admission
charge*
Ridderzaal
*Binnenhof 8A (tel: 070 364 6144).
Open: Monday to Saturday 10am–
4pm. Admission charge*
Rijksmuseum Mesdag
*Laan van Meerdevoort 7 (tel: 070 363
5450). Open: Tuesday to Saturday
10am–5pm, Sunday 1pm–5pm.
Admission charge*

Mauritshuis Museum at Den Haag

children but even more popular is the
Madurodam miniature town at
Haringkade 175, on the road to
Scheveningen; this is a fascinating 1:25
scale reproduction of Dutch landscape
features – towns, farms, the port of
Rotterdam and Schiphol airport.
Scheveningen itself, almost a suburb of
Den Haag, is a breezy North Sea coastal
resort. Its attractions include an
imposing Empire-style hotel and casino,
called the Kurhaus, a model of Jules
Verne's Nautilus submarine, good fish
restaurants and a long stretch of clean
sandy beach.
*Location: 60km southwest of Amsterdam
Getting there: train line 3 or 12 to Den
Haag HS (Hollands Spoor) station, then
change for Den Haag CS (Centraal
Station); journey time 35 minutes
Tourist information: Koningin Julianasplein
30, to the right of the station exit
(tel: 070 354 6200)*

Royalty

Den Haag is the home of the Dutch royal family and several operators offer 'royal tours' taking in the lovely 17th-century Huis ten Bosch (House in the Woods), where Queen Beatrix lives amidst extensive parkland to the east of the city.

Queen Beatrix was crowned on 30 April 1980 amidst great controversy. The planned festivities turned into a full-scale riot as protestors, objecting to the cost of the investiture and seeking to highlight the housing crisis, fought with police in Amsterdam. Since then Queen Beatrix has worked hard to sweep away the mystique of the monarchy. Though she is the second richest woman in Europe (after Queen Elizabeth II of Britain) she avoids ostentation, loves cycling in the countryside and has often said she would have been a social worker if she had not been queen. Her husband, Prince Claus, once

suffered from depression and won praise for talking about it publicly, thus giving help to others with a similar problem. By behaving like an ordinary modern family, the Dutch royals have overcome any lingering resentment about their privileged position.

Queen Beatrix also works with consummate professionalism to promote Dutch interests at home and abroad. Once asked to define her job she replied; 'The kingdom is something to be marketed, just like oranges', a humorous, if unintentional, reference to the fact that she is descended from the French House of Orange.

The Dutch are not monarchists at heart but the royal family has won their respect and affection – as can be seen when the whole country joins in the annual celebrations on 30 April in honour of Koninginnedag, the Queen's official birthday.

*Celebrations for Queen's
Day on 30 April*

*Queen Beatrix is the popular
head of a modern monarchy*

HAARLEM

Haarlem, the capital of Noord Holland province, is a mere 13 minutes from Amsterdam by train but a world away in atmosphere. Compared with the bustle of Amsterdam, Haarlem has a peaceful, almost rural, atmosphere, and it is a pleasure to wander through its quiet streets or along the banks of the River Spaarne which winds its way round the historic centre of the city.

Flowers for sale in Haarlem's Grote Markt

On arrival, the station itself is worth more than a passing glance; built in 1908, it is a stylish building of art deco tilework, honey-coloured woodwork and cast iron. Jansweg leads from the station to the magnificent Grote Kerk, begun in the 14th century and completed in the 16th. The church was a favourite subject of 17th-century painters and may already be familiar from pictures in Amsterdam's Rijksmuseum. The simple white-painted interior serves to highlight the mighty Christian Müller organ, one of the largest in the world, and its baroque ornamentation. Mozart (aged 10), Liszt and Saint-Saëns have all played at its keyboard and there are regular recitals during the week.

Many small shops cluster around the church walls; the one on the north side was built in 1603 as the Vishal (Fish Market). Alongside is the city's main square, Grote Markt, surrounded by notable buildings: the Renaissance Stadhuis, the Vleeshal (Meat Market) of 1603 with its giant ox-head carvings, and the Hoofdwacht (Guardhouse) of 1650. The statue by the church is of L J Coster to whom the Dutch attribute the invention of printing.

To the east of Grote Kerk, Damstraat leads past the Waag (Weighhouse) of 1598 to the River Spaarne and its pretty white bridge. Alongside is the Teylers Collection, founded in 1778 and preserved in its original state; it is full of beautifully crafted scientific instruments of polished wood and brass and cases of fossils. Also on display is a collection of drawings, including works by Michelangelo, Rembrandt and Raphael.

Returning to Grote Markt, head south down Warmoesstraat, Schangchelstraat and Groot Heiligland to reach the city's main attraction, the Frans Hals Museum. This is located in the Oudemannhuis, formerly a home for the elderly, built in 1608. Frans Hals was born in Antwerp but settled in Haarlem in the 1580s and, despite being one of the greatest portrait artists of his age, ended up an impoverished inmate of this same institution.

The museum has eight of the artist's large group paintings, including one of the governors of the home, painted when Frans Hals was over 80, but quite evidently still in full possession of his

The ornate interior of St Bavo's Church

good concentration of antique shops leading up to the 17th-century Nieuwekerk. From here, either take Lange Annastraat north to see the 17th-century *hofjes* (almshouses) that line either side, or walk back up the main shopping street, Grote Houtstraat. In Grote Markt you can rest your feet at one of several popular pavement cafés and there are more characterful shops on Kruistraat, leading back to the station.
Location: 23km west of Amsterdam
Getting there: train line 7 or 12; journey time 13 minutes
Tourist information: Stationsplein 1 (tel: 023 319 059)

Frans Hals Museum
Groot Heiligland 62 (tel: 023 319 180). Open March to September, Tuesday to Saturday 10am–5pm, Sunday 1pm–5pm; October to February, Tuesday to Saturday 10am–4pm, Sunday 1pm–4pm. Admission charge.
Grote Kerk
Oude Groenmarkt 23. Open: Monday to Saturday 10am–4pm. Admission charge.
Teylers Museum
Spaarne 16 (tel: 023 316 851). Open: March to September, Tuesday to Saturday 10am–5pm, Sunday 1pm–5pm; October to February, Tuesday to Saturday 10am–4pm, Sunday 1pm–4pm. Admission charge.

---

powers; the picture expresses something of the bitterness he must have felt as the recipient of charity from these stern-faced and reproachful burghers. Van Gogh admired the outstanding use of colour, counting no less than 27 different tones of black.

Another superbly realised picture shows the members of the Civic Guard of St Adrian at their annual banquet, flush-faced and evidently well into their cups. Their inebriated state is conveyed partly by the unflattering facial expressions but also by the way that Frans Hals has presented the ruffs, beards and ceremonial sashes at all sorts of tipsy angles – looking at the picture too long will make your own head begin to spin.

From the museum you can weave your way back to the Grote Markt through streets where time seems to have stood still and where several shops retain their original 18th- or 19th-century fittings. Kerkstraat has a particularly

The Frans Hals Museum

The unique charm of Hoorn

HOORN

Hoorn was once a major port until cut off from the sea by the damming of the Zuider Zee (IJsselmeer). Several famous mariners were born here. J P Coen, whose statue is to be found in the main square, founded the colony of Batavia (better known today as Jakarta, the capital of Indonesia),Willem Schouten rounded the southern tip of the Americas in 1616 and named it Kap Hoorn (Cape Horn) after his native town, and Abel Tasman sailed from here to discover Tasmania and New Zealand.

The historic harbour quarter from where all these momentous voyages began is well preserved and lined with old warehouses. E V Lucas, the English travel writer, described the town in 1905 as 'rising from the sea like an enchanted city. . . its spires and harbour tower beautifully unreal'. That same view can be enjoyed in summer by taking a boat excursion into the IJsselmeer from the pier in front of the harbour tower, the Hoofdtoren, built in 1532 and given its spire in 1651.

In the town centre, Hoorn's main attraction is the Westfries Museum (Rode Steen 1). This occupies an ornate Mannerist building of 1632, built when Hoorn was capital of the now defunct West Friesland province and decorated with the coats of arms of the region's principal towns. The interiors evoke the splendours of the Golden Age with their 17th-century furnishings, costumes, toys and reconstructed shops. Rode Steen is also the venue for a craft fair every Wednesday in July and August at which costumed stallholders demonstrate traditional crafts such as lacemaking and clog carving.

Location: 37km north of Amsterdam
Getting there: train line to Enkhuizen;
journey time 37 minutes
Tourist information: Nieuwestraat 23
(tel: 02290 18342)
Open: Westfries Museum, Monday to
Friday 11am–5pm; Saturday, Sunday and
public holidays 2pm–5pm.

KEUKENHOF AND LISSE

Keukenhof is the showcase of the Dutch bulb industry, a 28-hectare park which erupts into riotous colour every year from late March to the end of May. This spectacle, described as 'the greatest flower show on earth' attracts half a million visitors but the park is big enough to accommodate them all (not so the cafés, however, which get crowded – wise visitors bring a picnic with them). The wooded park is threaded by a 16km network of paths and the potentially garish effect of millions of bulbs is mitigated by skilful planting; variety is provided by the soft green of the woodland putting out new leaves early in the season, followed by the snowy blossoms of Japanese cherry trees and, later in the year, by masses of azalea and rhododendron blooms. The peak of the season occurs at the end of April when there is a huge flower parade around the streets of the nearby town of Lisse.

Keukenhof is located in the heart of the *bollenstreek*, the bulb-growing strip, which stretches from Haarlem south to Leiden. This compact area can be explored by bicycle from Leiden, Harlem or Lisse using maps available from VVV Tourist Information Centres. The cycleways are well marked but can be crowded, especially at weekends. The bulbfields are a spectacular but shortlived sight; commercial growers allow the bulbs to flower just long enough to check that they are true to colour and free from virus and disease. The flowers are then picked, or even mown off, so that the bulb uses its energies in growing bulblets rather than seed.

The fascinating history of bulb culture in The Netherlands is covered by the Museum voor Bloemnebollenstreek in Lisse *(Heereweg 219)*. Here visitors can learn about modern hi-tech production techniques and about the tulip mania that gripped the country after the first bulbs began to be imported from Turkey from 1630; speculation in rare varieties led to massive fortunes being won and lost.

Location: 32km southwest of Amsterdam
Getting there: scores of operators compete to offer coach excursions to Keukenhof and the bulbflelds and these can be booked at the VVV Tourist Information Centre in Amsterdam. Alternatively you can buy a day-trip ticket from Amsterdam Centraal station which includes bus transfers from Haarlem and admission charges.
Tourist information: Lisse, Grachtweg 53A (tel: 02521 19034)
Open: Keukenhof, late March to end of May, daily 8am–6.30pm; Bloemenbollenstreek Museum, April and May, daily 10am–5pm, rest of year Tuesday to Saturday 1pm–5pm, Sunday 11.30am–5pm.

The bulb-growing heart of The Netherlands

LEIDEN

Leiden is a likeable university town whose numerous museums will fill a full day. The university, the oldest in The Netherlands, was founded in 1574 by William the Silent as a reward for the town's stoicism in the face of a year-long siege by the Spanish. The siege ended only when William broke the dykes around the town enabling his ships to sail up to the walls on the resulting floodwaters. When the Spanish retreated the starving citizens climbed the ramparts to find an abandoned iron pot full of spicy beef and vegetable stew; this same dish, *hutspot,* has become the town's culinary speciality.

The university became a major centre of learning and the town still has a studious atmosphere, though its several museums are far from stuffy.

The **Stedelijk Museum de Lakenhal** *(Oude Singel 28)* is a short walk from the station and covers the history of Leiden and especially its cloth weaving industry, the staple of the local economy until the 18th century. The museum's best-known painting is Lucas van Leyden's *Last Judgement* triptych and there are numerous rooms furnished

Still life with windmill at Leiden

in period style, including a kitchen and brewery.

Nearly opposite *(on Tweede Binnenvestgracht 1)* is the **Molenmuseum de Valk,** an eight-storey windmill built in 1743 and still in working order. This absorbing museum covers the history of windmills in The Netherlands and provides panoramic views of the city.

A third museum, the **Rijksmuseum voor Volkenkunde** (National Ethnology Museum) is a short stroll away *(Steenstraat 1)*. Here visitors plunge into the colourful world of Indonesian masks and puppets, Javanese sculpture and exquisite Japanese lacquer boxes, all deriving from Dutch colonial trade with the east.

Just south of the museum, on Morspoort, is another windmill, this time a replica of the mill owned by Rembrandt's father, Gerritszoon van Rijn. Rembrandtbrug crosses the River Rijn (Rhine) leading to Weedensteeg where Rembrandt was born in 1606.

By walking down Rembrandtstraat, left into picturesque Groeenhazebgracht, then right on Rapenburg, you will come to the university district with its handsome classical buildings, notably the Bibliotheca Thysiana of 1655.

Ethnic treasures at the National Ethnology Museum

Further down is the entrance to **Hortus Botanicus** *(the Botanical Garden, Rapenburg 73)* founded in 1575. This delightful spot includes a reconstruction of the original garden, the Clusiustuin, named after the garden's former director, Carolus Clusius, the botanist who first introduced bulbs to The Netherlands.

Another famous Leiden citizen is buried in **St Pieterskerk**, on the opposite side of Rapenburg. He is John Robinson, a Puritan refugee from England who settled in Leiden in 1609. He became the leader of the Pilgrim Fathers who set sail from Rotterdam in 1620, bound for a new life in the New World. Robinson himself was too ill to join that pioneering voyage and died not long after.

St Pieterskerk is surrounded by the narrow lanes of the medieval quarter, lined by bookshops and peaceful cafés. To the east, Pieterskerkchoorsteeg leads to the main street, Breestraat, and the Renaissance Stadhuis of 1595. To the north, Pieterskerkhof leads to the attractive jumble of buildings that make up Gravensteen, once the court and prison, now the Law Faculty.

Back on Rapenburg you will find the popular **Rijksmuseum van Oudheden** (The National Archaeological Museum).

An ancient Egyptian temple has been reconstructed at the entrance to the museum, given to the Dutch nation by the Egyptian government. The Temple of Taffeh was originally built in the 1st century AD for the worship of the sun and converted to Christian use in the 4th century. The museum has a big collection of Egyptian and Roman material and, less glamorous but of greater local relevance, a floor devoted to the archaeology of The Netherlands.

Location: 42km southwest of Amsterdam
Getting there: train line 3 or 12; journey time 30 minutes
Tourist information: Stationsplein 210 (tel: 071 146 846)

Hortus Botanicus
Rapenburg 73. Open: May to September, Monday to Friday 8.30am–5.30pm, Sunday 2pm–5pm. Admission charge.
Molenmuseum de Valk Tweede
Binnenvestgracht 1 (tel: 071 254 639). Open: Tuesday to Saturday 10am–5pm, Sunday 1pm–5pm. Admission charge.
St Pieterskerk
Kloksteeg. Open: daily 1.30pm–4pm. Admission free.
Rijksmuseum van Oudheden
Rapenburg 28 (tel: 071 211 824). Open: Tuesday to Saturday 10am–5pm, Sunday 1pm–5pm. Admission charge.
Rijksmuseum voor Volkenkunde
Steenstraat 1 (tel: 071 211 824). Open: Tuesday to Saturday 10am–5pm, Sunday 1pm–5pm. Admission charge.
Stedelijk Museum de Lakenhal
Oude Singei 29 (tel: 071 254 620). Open: Tuesday to Saturday 10am–5pm, Sunday 1pm–5pm.

MARKEN

Of all the villages on the IJsselmeer north of Amsterdam, Marken is the quietest and most appealing. The local people have reluctantly turned to tourism to save their economy but they remain proud of their distinctive local traditions. Until 1957, Marken was an island, accessible only by boat, and the population of 200 formed an enclosed, strictly Calvinist community largely untouched by the modern world. The way of life of this fishing village began to change with the building of a causeway in 1957, providing a link to the mainland, and the population has been swelled by incomers to around 2,000.

Long isolation led to a distinctive style of architecture. The pristine wooden houses lining the harbour are a favourite subject for photographers; they are built on stilts as a flood precaution and linked by timber boardwalks. The clapboard façades are painted green and white, while bright red awnings and scarlet geraniums add to the colourful effect – even the boats moored in the harbour are painted in the same bright colours.

Local people still wear traditional

Visitors succumb easily to Marken's charm

Pottery is an important local industry

costume, especially on religious feast days, and a distinctive feature is the *ryglyf*, a bodice embroidered with intricate floral motifs. Marken has all the appearance of an open-air museum, but it is a living village of real atmosphere. Many visitors fall in love with its quiet charms, especially by contrast with the more commercialised village of Volendam, which can be reached from Marken by means of a half-hour boat trip.

Location: 18km northeast of Amsterdam
Getting there: Bus 11 from Amsterdam Centraal station or by boat, the Marken Express, from Volendam or Monnikendam, every 45 minutes during daylight hours from March to October
Tourist information: in Monnickendam, De Zarken 2 (tel: 02995 1998).

MUIDERSLOT

Muiderslot, also known as Muiden Castle, is a beautiful red-brick building that rises from its moat like the archetypal fairy-tale castle. It was originally built in 1285 by a count of Holland, Floris V, who set the economy of medieval Amsterdam on a sound footing by granting its citizens a 'toll privilege' in 1275; this enabled Amsterdammers to transport their goods along the canals of Holland county without paying tolls. Despite – or because of – this, Floris V was kidnapped, imprisoned and finally murdered in his own castle by a group of noblemen angered by his generosity, which had the effect of undermining their income.

The Bishop of Utrecht, who may have been behind the murder conspiracy, annexed the count's territory and demolished the castle in 1296. The castle was then rebuilt on the same foundations in 1386 and 300 years later it became the residence of Pieter Hooft. Between 1609 and 1647, Hooft, an

The turrets and battlements of Muiderslot Castle seem straight from a fairy-tale

illustrious poet and historian, used the castle as a place of philosophical and artistic debate. Here he would entertain the leading poets, artists and intellectuals of his day, who became known as the Muiden Circle.

After a period of neglect the castle was thoroughly restored in 1948 and it is now furnished in the style of the early 17th century, as it might have been in the time of Pieter Hooft. The charms of the castle are enhanced by delightful gardens.

Location: 12km east of Amsterdam (tel: 02942 1325)
Getting there: Bus 136, 137 or 138 from Amsterdam Amstel station; journey time 40 minutes
Open: April to September, Monday to Friday 10am–5pm, Sunday 1pm–5pm; October to March, Monday to Friday 10am–4pm, Sunday 1pm–4pm.
Guided tours, lasting an hour, begin on the hour.

MONNICKENDAM

Monnickendam has been described as Amsterdam in miniature. Though little more than a village today it has some remarkable buildings surviving from a time when Monnickendam was an important trading centre. The triple-naved **Grote Kerk** dates from the 15th century and has a fine oak choir screen

adapted and turned their hands to fish processing, specialising in smoked herrings and plump eels caught in the IJsselmeer. The fragrant smell of woodsmoke lingers in the harbour area where several old-fashioned and informal cafés serve the local speciality – *Monnickendammer twaalf uurtje,* a platter of delicately smoked fish. Another of the

Monnickendam was a busy merchant port

of 1563. In the narrow lanes of the harbour area, the 15th-century **Speeltoren**, or Clock Tower, now serves as the local museum; the original clockwork knights in white armour still parade on the hour when the clock carillon plays its delightful tune. Streets such as Burgwallen, Kerkstraat and Noordeinde are lined by attractive 17th-century houses built by prosperous merchants in the Golden Age.

Like other towns on the IJsselmeer, Monnickendam lost its outlet to the sea when the Zuider Zee was dammed, but the enterprising local people quickly

town's attractions is the Marken Express, a boat service linking the town with the nearby villages of Marken and Volendam; boats depart at 45-minute intervals from March to October.
*Location: 16km north of Amsterdam
Getting there: bus 111 from Amsterdam
Centraal station; journey time 30 minutes
Tourist information: De Zarken 2 (tel:
02995 1998)
Open: Museum, June to August, Monday
to Saturday 10.30am–4pm, Sunday
1.30pm–4pm.*

NAARDEN

Naarden suffered a devastating blow in 1572 when the town was sacked by Spanish troops under Don Frederick of Toledo (son of the Duke of Alva) and almost all the inhabitants were massacred. The brutality of the attack only increased Dutch determination to drive the hated Spaniards from their soil. Naarden was left a ghost town until repopulated in the 17th century when, in order to prevent the possibility of another massacre, the town was equipped with state-of-the-art defences, designed by Adriaan Dortsman. As a result Naarden now has some of the best-preserved Renaissance fortifications in Europe and the town resembles an island surrounded by an impressive double moat and bastions. Their story is told in the Vestingmuseum (Fortification Museum) located in the Turfpoortbastion *(Westwalstraat 6)*. This is no dry museum of military history but an excellent account of 17th-century warfare; there are subterranean passages to explore and the admission price includes a boat trip around the moats.

The massacre of 1572 is commemorated by a plaque on the Spaanse Huis *(Spanish House, Turfpoortstraat 27)*, built in 1615. This now houses the Comeniusmuseum, devoted to the life and theories of the philosopher, Johann Komenski (Comenius), a Moravian refugee who settled in the town in 1621 and laid the foundations of modern educational practice; he abhorred learning by rote and was a pioneering advocate of 'visual aids'.

The Grote Kerk, in the centre of the town, fortunately survived the Spanish onslaught. It has a wooden choir screen of 1513 and an unusual set of vault paintings illustrating stories from the Old and New Testaments; the 20 wooden panels, painted between 1510 and 1518, are based on the woodcuts of Dürer. The tower is well worth climbing for a bird's-eye view of the fortifications and of the surrounding Gooiland landscape, an extensive area of woodland, heath and lakes. The television tower visible in the distance is located in the Amsterdam suburb of Hilversum, headquarters of the Dutch national broadcasting company.

Location: 21km east of Amsterdam
Getting there: Bus 136, 137 or 138 from Amsterdam Amstel station; journey time 55 minutes
Tourist information: Adriaan Dortsmanplein 1B (tel: 021 594 2836)
Open: Vestingmuseum, end of March to October, Monday to Friday 10am–4.30pm, Saturday and Sunday 12 noon–5pm; Grote Kerk, May to September, Saturday to Thursday 2pm–4pm; Comeniusmuseum, Tuesday to Sunday 2pm–5pm.

The tranquillity of modern-day Naarden belies a violent past

ROTTERDAM

Rotterdam was virtually flattened at the beginning of World War II when the Nazis bombed The Netherlands into surrender. A new city has arisen on the old, noted for its imaginative modern architecture, its excellent museums and for the world's largest container port.

Shapes of today in rebuilt Rotterdam...

The rather soulless city centre is the least attractive part. From the station cross to the windswept pedestrian shopping mall either side of Coolsingel; putting this behind, it is best to head for the waterfront around **Oude Haven** where the most striking of the city's buildings are located. The pyramidal **Gemeentebibliotheeek** (Central Library) clearly owes a debt to the Pompidou Centre in Paris with its external ducting and polished steel. Take a ride on the escalators for views over the old port and of the internal hanging gardens. Alongside are the unusual cube houses designed by Piet Blom; one of them, the **Kijk Kubus** *(Overblaak 70)* is open to the public and well worth a visit even if you conclude that the giddying wall angles and the specially adapted furniture make these futuristic houses rather a strain to live in. The complex includes a shop-lined bridge based on the Ponte Vecchio in Florence and the wharf is lined with pleasant cafés.

Further along the boat-filled harbour you will find the **Maritime Museum Prins Hendrik**, devoted to the city's long maritime history. The *Museumschip Buffel*, moored alongside, is a 19th-century warship with surprisingly luxurious officers' quarters.

If you continue down Leuvehaven you will come to the harbour-side offices of Spido Havenrondvaarten, the departure point for boat tours of the Europoort. Further along the waterfront is a distinguished classical building, formerly the Royal Netherlands Yacht Club, now a museum of geography and ethnography, the **Museum voor Land en Volkenkunde**.

Towering above the adjacent park is the **Euromast**, built in 1960 for the Floriade flower festival and originally 100m high. The Space Tower was added subsequently bringing the total height to 183m. External lifts climb to the revolving Space Cabin at the summit

... and shapes of yesterday at Delfsharen

THE EUROPOORT

Rotterdam's Europoort stretches for 37km along the Nieuwe Maas river and handles some 4 per cent of the world's container traffic. Cargo unloaded here is transported deep into the heart of Europe along three great rivers, the Rhine, the Maas (Meuse) and the Scheldt. Every year around 32,000 ships dock and unload their containers – laid end to end they would stretch for 563,200km. These and other overwhelming statistics come to life if you take one of the 75-minute Spido harbour tours which depart from Willemsplein regularly during the day *(tel: 010 413 5400)*.

Dubbelde Palmboom Museum
Voorhaven 10 (tel: 010 476 1533).
Open: Tuesday to Saturday 10am–5pm, Sunday 11am–5pm. Admission charge.

Euromast
Parkhaven 20 (tel: 010 436 4811).
Open: January and February, Saturday and Sunday 11am–4pm; March to September, daily 10am– 9pm; October to December, daily 11am–4pm. Admission charge.

Kijk Kubus
Overblaak 70 (tel: 010 414 2285).
Open: January to March Saturday and Sunday 11am–5pm; April, May and October to December, Tuesday to Sunday 11am–5pm; June to September daily 10am–5pm. Admission charge.

Maritiem Museum Prins Hendrik
Leuvehaven (tel: 010 413 2680). Open: Tuesday to Saturday 10am– 5pm, Sunday 11am–5pm. Admission charge.

Museum Boymans-Van Beuningen
Mathenesserlaan 18 (tel: 010 441 9400). Open: Tuesday to Saturday 10am–5pm, Sunday 11am–5pm. Admission charge.

Museum voor Land en Volkenkunde
Willemskade 25 (tel: 010 411 1055). Open: Tuesday to Saturday 10am–5pm, Sunday 11am–5pm. Admission charge.

where the views take in the whole 37km waterfront of the Europoort.

Totally different in scale is the Delfshaven district alongside, which escaped bombing and is lined with 18th- and 19th-century warehouses converted to chic apartments. The Pilgrim Fathers sailed from here in 1620 in the *Speedwell;* this ship proved unseaworthy and so, after docking at the English port of Plymouth, the religious refugees continued their voyage to the New World in the *Mayflower*. The Dubbelde Palmboom Museum *(Voorhaven 12)* explains the history of the area and its industries.

Returning to the city centre, the Museum Boymans-van Beuningen *(Mathenesserlaan 18–20)* contains one of Europe's most important art collections. Three sections of this vast museum are a must: the rooms dedicated to early Dutch painting contain Pieter Bruegel's *Tower of Babel* and several works by Hieronymus Bosch; rooms 36 and 37 are devoted to the work of Rembrandt and his pupils; rooms 25 to 30 contain a comprehensive collection of Surrealistic paintings, including well-known works by Dali, Magritte and Ernst.

Location: 76km southwest of Amsterdam
Getting there: train line 3; journey time 60 minutes
Tourist information: Coolsingel 67 (tel: 010 413 6000)

UTRECHT

Utrecht is one of the oldest cities in The Netherlands, founded in AD47 as a Roman garrison town to protect a strategic ford across the River Rhine. Pepin the Short, father of Charlemagne, made Utrecht a bishopric in the 7th century and the city became the main religious centre of the northern Dutch provinces in the Middle Ages, its skyline bristling with the spires of numerous churches and convents. Many were destroyed by a hurricane that hit the town in 1674. Those that remain range in style from Romanesque to High Gothic, several of them now converted to museums.

On arriving in Utrecht visitors first have to negotiate the intrusive 1970s Hoog Catharijne office and shopping complex which stands between the station and the old city. Head for **Oude Gracht**, an unusual sunken canal built in two tiers to accommodate the tidal extremes of the Rhine. The lower quay is lined with cavernous cellars, many now turned into cafés and restaurants. Some of Utrecht's oldest buildings line the canal; the Huis Oudaen (no 99) dates from 1320 and Drakenborch (no 114) was built in 1280.

Follow the canal south heading for the unmissable landmark of the **Domtoren** (Cathedral Tower), a lacy Gothic masterpiece completed in 1382 and soaring to 112m. Some contemporaries dismissed the tower as a symbol of vanity and pride, predicting that it would surely collapse. In fact it was the cathedral which came crashing to the ground in the 1674 hurricane, leaving only the choir of 1321, modelled on Cologne Cathedral, and the 15th-century cloister.

The cathedral was conceived as the

The sunken canal at Oude gracht

centrepiece of an ambitious scheme devised by Bishop Bernold in the mid-11th century. He drew up a plan to build five churches, one at each of the four cardinal points of the compass and the cathedral in the centre, together forming the shape of the cross. Only two of the five were completed in Bernold's lifetime: to the east of the Domkerk is **Pieterskerk**, built in Romanesque style in 1048, while to the north is **Janskerk**, completed in 1050 and given a new Gothic choir in the 16th century.

From Janskerk, follow the canal delightfully called Drift and then turn left down Kromme Nieuwegracht; this canal follows the original course of the Rhine and is lined with elegant 18th-century houses. It leads to picturesque Pausdam and the late-Gothic **Paushuisje** (Pope's House), built in 1517 for Adriaan Floriszoon. He never saw the house, having spent most of his time in Spain as tutor to Charles V and then as the Bishop of Tortosa. In 1622 he became Adrian VI, the first and only Dutch pope – a short-lived reign as he died the following year.

Nieuwegracht leads south to a former Carmelite convent, now the **Rijksmuseum het Catherijneconvent**, whose excellent medieval paintings and sculptures are part of a collection illustrating the history of religion in The Netherlands. Further south, the Centraal Museum, housed in another medieval convent, has an eclectic range of exhibits, ranging from period rooms, costumes and doll's houses, to the Renaissance paintings of Utrecht artist, Jan van Scorel, and the colourful modern furniture of the de Stijl movement architect, Gerrit Rietveld. Train enthusiasts should not miss the **Spoorweg (Railway) Museum**, housed near by in the disused 19th-century station.

The best route back to the city centre is through the park alongside Stadsbuitengracht, formerly the moat of the medieval city walls, then up Sprinweg to Buurkerk. This 13th-century church now houses the Muscum van Speelklok tot Pierement (meaning From Musical Clocks to Street Organs), an enchanting museum of mechanical musical instruments.

Location: 35km south of Amsterdam
Getting there: train line 5 or 7 from Amsterdam Centraal station; journey time 30 minutes
Tourist information: Vredenburg 90 (tel: 030 314 132)

Centraal Museum
Agnietenstraat (tel: 030 315 541).
Open: Tuesday to Saturday 10am–5pm, Sunday 1pm–5pm. Admission charge.

Domtoren
Domplein (tel: 030 919 540). Open: April to October, Monday to Friday 10am–5pm, Saturday and Sunday 12 noon–5pm. Admission charge.

Museum van Speelklok tot Pierement
Buurkerkhof 10 (tel: 030 312 789).
Open: Tuesday to Saturday 10am–4pm, Sunday 1pm–4pm. Admission charge.

Nederlands Spoorwegmuseum
Oldenbarneveltlaan 6 (tel: 030 318 514). Open: Tuesday to Saturday 10am–5pm, Sunday 1pm–5pm. Admission charge.

Rijksmuseum het Catherijneconvent
Nieuwe Gracht 63 (tel: 030 313 835).
Open: Tuesday to Friday 10am–5pm, Saturday and Sunday 1pm–5pm. Admission charge.

The imposing Kasteel de Haar is a Utrecht landmark

Souvenirs for sale in Volendam

VOLENDAM

The former fishing village of Volendam is now a highly commercialised tourist attraction, to be avoided by those who do not like crowds and shops full of kitsch souvenirs (go to quieter Marken or Monnickendam instead). On the other hand it is fun for children and the local people are friendly, wholehearted participants in this recreation of 'old world' Holland. Like actors in a living theme park, they pose for photographers in village costume – baggy black trousers for the men and winged lace caps, flowered dresses and striped aprons for the women. Visitors are also welcome to dress up in costume and have their pictures taken. The harbour is lined with picturesque wooden houses, no two alike, and the **Volendam Museum** (*Kloostervuurt 5*) tells the story of the ups and downs of the local fishing industry.
Location: 18km northeast of Amsterdam
Getting there: bus 110 from Amsterdam

Centraal station (journey time 30 minutes) or by day-trip excursion ticket which includes the rail journey to Edam plus bus and boat transfers to Marken and Volendam
Tourist information: Zeestraat 21 (tel: 02993 63747)
Open: museum, April to October, daily 10am–5pm.

ZAANSE SCHANS

The former villages of Zaandam, Koog aan de Zaan and Zaandijk, north of Amsterdam, all take their names from the River Zaan on whose banks they sit. An industrial revolution of a kind occurred here in the 16th century with the invention of a wind-powered sawmill; the area became the biggest supplier of timber for shipbuilding and house construction in The Netherlands. When Monet came here to paint the scene in the 1870s there were over

The national footwear as worn in Zaanse Schans

1,000 windmills producing everything from corn and mustard to paint pigments and vegetable oil. Development has continued and the former villages have merged to form the Zaanstad conurbation. In the 1950s many of the surviving windmills were moved to an open-air museum called Zaanse Schans, located on the river bank opposite Zaandijk. An unusual feature of the museum is that people actually live in its houses and windmills, and several of the mills continue to produce mustard and flour. They are maintained in pristine working order by enthusiasts who are dedicated to keeping traditional milling skills alive and who lovingly demonstrate the complex workings of these elegant 'machines'. The museum also has several streets of 17th-century timber-gabled houses where visitors can watch craft demonstrations, and take a boat trip along the River Zaan.
Location: 14km north of Amsterdam
Getting there: train from Amsterdam Centraal station to Koog-Zandijk; journey time 15 minutes
Tourist information: Zaandam, Gedemplegracht 76 (tel: 075 162 221)
Open: April to November, daily 10am–5pm

ZANDVOORT

On hot summer days when Amsterdammers feel like a cooling dip in the sea they head for Zandvoort, a popular coastal resort but big enough to accommodate the crowds with ease. The busiest beaches are those closest to Zandvoort town, whose northern quarter has been conserved and retains the atmosphere of a fishing village. The modern part of the town has numerous fish restaurants, a dolphinarium *(Burgermeester van Fenemaplein 2)* and a casino (Badhuisplaats) worth a visit just

for the views. Sandy and gently shelving beaches stretch for miles either side of the town and you will find privacy if you walk far enough.

Nature lovers should head south to the **Waterliedingduinen**, an undulating dune reserve where horned poppy and sea holly grow in the sheltered lee of the shifting sandbanks.
Location: 25km west of Amsterdam
Getting there: train from Amsterdam Centraal station to Zandvoort aan Zee; journey time 24 minutes
Tourist information: Schoolplein 1 (tel: 02507 17947)

One of the working windmills at Zaanse Schans open-air museum

ZUIDERZEE MUSEUM, ENKHUIZEN

The Zuiderzee Museum in Enkhuizen tells the fascinating story of the reclamation of the Zuider Zee and of the vanished way of life of its former fishing villages. Drainage of the Zuider Zee began as early as the 17th century with the creation of the Beemster, Purmer and Wormer polders. Dykes were built to hold back the sea, and drainage canals were dug; windmills, fitted with scoop wheels, were then used to raise the water high enough to flow back into the sea. The land thus reclaimed was very fertile;

Vanished lives are recreated at the Zuiderzee Museum

villages surrounding the Zuider Zee became wealthy on the profits from arable crops, adding to their income from marine trade and fishing, and they built imposing town halls to celebrate their new prosperity.

By the mid-18th century, the sea had silted up to the extent that big ships could no longer reach Amsterdam, a problem resolved by digging the Noordzee Kanaal, which opened in 1876. The widespread use of steam pumps from the mid-19th century added impetus to land reclamation, but the new fields were always liable to flooding from the combined forces of high tides and heavy rainfall. After a devastating flood that occurred in 1916, a long-standing plan to dam the Zuider Zee, first mooted by the engineer Cornelis Lely in 1891, was revived. The Afsluitdijk (Enclosing Dyke) was built by sinking woven willow mattresses to act as a raft, thus preventing the huge weight of stones and concrete piled on top from sinking into the sea bed. When the dyke was completed in 1932, flags flew at half mast in the port towns round the shore, now cut off from the sea.

The old tidal Zuider Zee became a shallow inland lake and was rechristened the IJsselmeer. By subdividing the lake with further dams, huge areas of marshland were drained and seeded with grass to draw off the salt before being turned over to agriculture. In this way the new province of Flevoland was created and its capital, named Lelystadt after the 19th-century engineer, received its first settlers in 1967.

Enkhuizen was one of the ports to suffer from an abrupt end to its former way of life; it had once been the foremost herring port in The Netherlands. As compensation for the loss of income, it was chosen as the site for the splendid Zuiderzee Museum – two museums, in fact, consisting of the indoor Binnenmuseum, opened in 1950, and the open-air Buitenmuseum, opened in 1983.

The Binnenmuseum is located in a splendid Renaissance building built on the waterfront in 1625 and known as the Peperhuis because, under East India Company ownership, it had been used for storing pepper imported from Indonesia. Room 1 of the museum houses a collection of historic Zuider Zee fishing boats, rooms 4 to 7 are devoted to locally made furniture and rooms 13 to 15 to traditional costume. It is clear from the exhibits that each village developed its own distinctive style, not just in dress but even in shipbuilding techniques, a reflection of the fact that these villages, though only a few miles apart, were rivals for trade and emphasised their differences in numerous ways.

The open-air museum is, appropriately enough, reached by boat which passes among the traditional sailing craft moored in the harbour. The museum consists of 130 buildings reconstructed to form complete streets modelled on the towns from which they were rescued; thus you can walk from Monnickendam to Edam, from Edam to Amsterdam and from the city to the more rural village of Staveren in the course of a few hours. Informative labelling explains the history of each building and its former occupants. Many are furnished in period style or used to demonstrate crafts, such as baking, herring curing, tanning and rope making.

If the museums do not keep you occupied for a whole day, you can always take a boat trip from the harbour (summer only) to **Medemblik**, with its steam train museum and 13th-century castle, or to Urk, with its Visserijmuseum (Fishing Museum) and excellent fish restaurants.

Location: 64km northeast of Amsterdam
Getting there: train from Amsterdam
Centraal station to Enkhuizen; journey time 60 minutes
Tourist information: Stationsplein 1 (tel: 02280 13164)
Open: 1 April to 21 October, daily 10am–5pm.

Herrings hung for smoking

Getting away from it all

AMSTERDAMSE BOS

Amsterdam Wood, located in the southern fringes of the city, is the product of the Great Depression of the 1930s. To resolve the problem of mass unemployment the city decided to convert 80 hectares of polder into a recreation park modelled on the Bois de Boulogne in Paris. The use of machinery was ruled out in the interests of creating the maximum number of jobs, so the park is man made in a very real sense; teams of men and horses laid 310km of drainage pipe to lower the water table by 1.5m so that the thousands of trees they planted would develop strong roots. They dug the 2km rowing lake, the Roeibaan, and created an artificial hill from the spoil to act as a viewpoint; they also laid over 200km of footpaths and cycle tracks.

The result today is a mature park, beautifully maintained, where visitors can escape the crowds and wander along

A rural idyll made by hand in Amsterdam Wood

tree-shaded paths, picnic in sunny glades or by the lakeside, hire a bicycle, go canoeing or swim in the lake. Those who simply want to walk can follow the Roeibaan to its furthest point and visit the Bosmuseum which explains how the park was built and illustrates all its flora and fauna, from squirrels and songbirds to fungi and 700 different beetle species.

Entrance: Van Nijenrodeweg
(museum tel: 643 1414)
Open: park 24 hours; museum daily
10am–5pm
Admission free
Bus 170, 171 or 172. Alternatively take tram 6 or 16, or bus 15, to Harlemmermeer station and ride to the park on an old-fashioned tram (services every Sunday April to October; see Electrisch Tramlijn Museum for details)
Nearby: Hortus Botanicus van de Vrije Universiteit.

HORTUS BOTANICUS PLANTAGE

Amsterdam's tiny Botanical Garden was laid out in 1638 as a medicinal garden, but it soon evolved into a showcase for the many new plants brought back by explorers from the Far East. The main features of the garden are a Palm House of iron and glass with aerial walkways, an Orangery, a herb garden in the 17th-century style and a Japanese garden. In recent years the gardens have had a neglected air but restoration is under way (so some areas may be closed off). The result should be a much improved collection with new greenhouses for tropical and desert plants, a restaurant and study centre.

Plantage Middenlaan 2 (tel: 625 8411)
Open: April to October, Monday to Friday
9am–5pm, Saturday, Sunday and public
holidays 11am–5pm; rest of year, Monday
to Friday 9am–4pm, Saturday, Sunday
and public holidays 11am–4pm
Admission charge
Trams 7, 9 or 14
Nearby: Zoo

HORTUS BOTANICUS VAN DE VRIJE UNIVERSITEIT

The Botanical Garden of the Free University was planted in 1967. It has an interesting section devoted to the native flora of The Netherlands, large areas of woodland planted with hardy shrubs and perennials, one of the largest fern collections in the world and glasshouses devoted to cold, temperate and tropical-climate plants.

Van der Boechorststraat 8 (tel: 548 4142)
Open: Monday to Friday 8am–4.30pm
Admission free
Buses 23, 65, 170, 171, 172 or 173
Nearby: Amsterdamse Bos

An ambitious development programme will make the Botanical Garden even more of a must for green-minded visitors

CYCLE ROUTES

Every year thousands of visitors to Amsterdam are seduced into believing that 'cycling is the ideal means of transport in Amsterdam'. They hire a bike and then wish they had not. Cycling in Amsterdam is a hair-raising experience; bike-riding natives are a law unto themselves, everybody seems to ignore the traffic rules, including pedestrians, and when you reach for your brakes you often find they are not there – many Dutch bikes are the old-fashioned kind which you have to back pedal to stop. Bicycles are also a favourite target of thieves who find ways of removing even the most securely locked bikes. With practice all these problems can be overcome, but if you do choose to cycle in Amsterdam, dismount at busy intersections and cross on foot and secure your bike to an immovable object if you leave it in the street.

By contrast, cycling in the Dutch countryside is a joy, especially in summer when there is no wind to fight against. The rider has the choice of over 10,000km of specially designated cycle paths *(fietspaden)*, which are clearly marked on ANWB 1:100,000 scale maps and well signposted on the ground. Road and cycleway intersections are usually numbered so you can always find out where you are on the map. VVV Tourist Information Centres also supply informative maps of local cycle routes. You can hire bicycles at almost any railway station – a system designed to discourage people from taking their own bikes on the trains. Simply present your ticket (which secures a small discount) and some means of identification, such as a passport, at the ticket office; you will be charged a small refundable deposit and a negligible hire fee; bikes with child seats can also be hired.

Several nature reserves within easy reach of Amsterdam offer traffic-free cycling conditions, as well as scenic

Cycling is an ideal way to reach and enjoy villages like Marken

landscapes, picnic spots and wildlife. From the station at Castricum (26km northwest of Amsterdam; journey time 30 minutes) you are within easy reach of the **North Holland Dunes Reserve**, an extensive area of sand and shingle bank backed by thick woodland. Johanna's Hof, at the highest point in the woods, is a popular destination for its pancakes and small zoo.

To the east of Amsterdam you can take a train to Hilversum (20km; journey time 20 minutes) and explore the extensive heath and woodland of the **Bussummerheide reserve**, heading for the pancake houses in the village of Lage Vuursche when you are hungry.

The rolling hills and moors of the **Hoge Veluwe National Park**, north of Arnhem (see **Amsterdam Environs** section) are ideal for cycling and free bikes, painted white, are available for anyone to use within the confines of the vast park. Hoge Veluwe has the added attraction of its open-air **sculpture park** and the **Kröller-Müller Museum**, featuring over 200 Van Gogh paintings.

Once confident enough to cope with the roads, you could visit the IJsselmeer villages of Marken and Monnickendam by bike instead of by bus or coach (maps available from the Amsterdam VVV). If you hire a bike at Amsterdam Centraal station you can cross the IJ harbour by free passenger ferry. The ferry departs regularly from the harbour side of the station (signposted Pont naar Tolhuis). You will initially encounter traffic on the northern bank but, as you cycle east along Durgerdammerdijk, the suburbs give way to open countryside dotted with red-roofed farmhouses and you may spot herons wading in the watercourses. The route passes through Durgerdam, an attractive former fishing village, then

The humble bicycle has found its niche in the flat, narrow streets, alleys and bridges of Amsterdam

along the shores of the IJsselmeer to Uitdam. Three kilometres further on is the causeway to the island village of Marken with its painted wooden houses and beyond lies **Monnickendam**, 'Amsterdam in miniature' (for both see **Amsterdam Environs**). The return journey passes through Broek in Waterland, a town of spotless beauty and a major centre of cheese production, where the informal restaurant, De Witte Swaen, is used for catering to hungry cyclists. From here the road through Zunderdorp will bring you back to the IJ ferry – allow at least four hours for the 34km round trip.

Cost effective, 'green' family transport

DEN HELDER AND THE WADDENZEE

From Amsterdam Centraal station it is only an hour by train to Den Helder, a port town on the edge of a truly wild corner of The Netherlands, renowned for its bird and marine life. Ferries from Den Helder cross to the island of Texel, the first and largest of the five Frisian (or Wadden) Islands which extend in a broad curve eastwards to the German coast. These islands, and the submerged sandbars in between, act as a natural breakwater, separating the shallow waters of the Waddenzee to the east from the rough and often stormy North Sea to the west.

The Waddenzee covers an area of almost 2,600sq km, but is nowhere more than 3m deep, even at high tide. As the tide goes out the sea rolls away to exposean extensive area of mudflats rich in marine molluscs, worms and the spawn of numerous North Sea fish. This in turn attracts huge feeding flocks of gulls, waders and wildfowl.

Den Helder itself was a fishing village

Maritime exhibits in the Rykers Museum at Den Helder

until Napoleon fortified it as a naval base in 1808, and it remains the headquarters of the Dutch naval fleet. Ferries to Texel depart from the harbour at hourly intervals all through the year and the crossing takes 20 minutes.

From the island port of 't Horntje buses go to Den Burg, the main village, where visitors can hire bicycles, see the local museum and then call at the VVV Tourist Information Centre *(Groenplats, tel: 02220 14741)* for a guide to cycle routes and to the island's numerous bird sanctuaries. De Hoog, on the western side of Texel, is the island's main resort and has a small natural history museum, the Ecomare, but the best spots for birdwatching lie to the south and east, below Den Hoorn. Depending on the time of year, visitors should look out for waders such as curlews, oystercatchers, plovers, redshanks, greenshanks and stints, as well as pintail ducks, shelducks, teal,

ISLAND HOPPING AND MUDWALKING

The best way to explore the Frisian islands is by hiring an antique sailboat for the week or a weekend, complete with crew and sleeping accommodation (details from Rederij *Vooruit Holland, tel: 0909 5155 1485*). Otherwise the islands can only be reached by separate ferries from the mainland. You can also walk to some of the islands on *wadlopen* (mudwalking) excursions during the summer months – but you must be prepared to get extremely muddy and be physically fit; wading up to your thighs in mud is as demanding as mountain climbing. It is far too dangerous to cross the mudflats on your own, but you can join a party led by an officially licensed guide if you want a close encounter with the rich and varied ecology of the Waddenzee (details from VVV Tourist Information Centres in *Dokkum, tel: 05190 3800; Leeuwarden, tel: 058 132 224;* and *Groningen, tel: 050 139 700*).

As a rule, the five Frisian islands become smaller, wilder and more remote from civilisation the further north you travel, although they can be busy on summer weekends when sunbathers and windsurfers pour out of the cities to enjoy them.

Texel is the only island where visitors will encounter cars in any number. Vlieland (reached by ferry from Harlingen) is popular with birdwatchers and naturists – it has the biggest nudist beach in Europe. Terschelling, the middle island (also reached from Harlingen) once guarded the main shipping lanes into the Zuider Zee; numerous ships were wrecked on its shifting sandbanks, including the *Lutine*, whose bell, the only part recovered, is still rung at Lloyd's, the London insurance market, whenever a ship is lost at sea.

terns and geese. Sadly the grey seals that were once so common are now a rare sight. A viral disease has decimated the population and the remaining colonies are now limited to the less-populated of the Frisian islands.

Mudlarks off on the trail

Shopping

*A*msterdam, a city built on commerce, seems at first glance to have surprisingly few shops, until you realise that they are, very sensibly, tucked away on pedestrianised side streets or along the short radial canals that link the three main canals of the Grachtengordel. Here you will find all sorts of surprises: Amsterdam's shopkeepers are masters of the art of window display and there are many small speciality shops that sell a single product in all its varieties – candles, condoms, cheeses, terracotta pots for the garden, handmade toys and greetings cards, not to mention flowers in profusion, made up into striking and irresistible bouquets. It is easy to spend a whole day shopping or browsing and not become bored. Thursday is best because the shops stay open until 9pm; Saturday is the busiest day but shops close promptly at 5pm and many do not open again until 1pm on Monday; the Calvinist heritage ensures that Sunday trading is strictly prohibited, and few shops are open on Monday morning. Otherwise normal shopping hours are between 9am and 6pm, and most major credit cards are universally accepted.

SHOPPING IN THE CENTRE

Damrak, the main street, is dominated by bureaux de change, fast-food outlets and souvenir shops, but **Allert de Lange**, *Damrak 62*, is an oasis of civilisation, stocking a good range of books in several European languages. Further up, **De Bijenkorf** (The Beehive) is the Harrods of Amsterdam selling everything from Delftware to handmade chocolates, though you may find certain goods cheaper at the C & A and Peek & Cloppenburg department stores on Dam Square.

Parallel to Damrak is Nieuwendijk, a crowded pedestrian precinct lined with cheap clothes shops and brightly lit stalls selling doughnuts and nougat that would not look out of place in a fairground.

Just behind Nieuwe Kerk, on *Nieuwezijds Voorburgwal 137–139*, is a delightful shop which captures the magic of Christmas even in the heat of summer; **Christmas World** sells

The Beehive is a honeypot for shoppers

nothing but old-fashioned tree decorations, stocking fillers and toys. Opposite, the former main Post Office is being turned into an up-market 200-shop galleria and promises to provide a new shopping focus to the city.

Kalverstraat, the main shopping street, runs from Dam square to Muntplein. Competition between traders is fierce and there are many bargains to be had if you shop around in the high street fashion stores. The American Discount Book Center, *no 185*, has a huge stock of paperbacks and children's books at genuine bargain prices. Several well-known multi-national chains also have branches here: Marks & Spencer at the corner of St Luciensteeg, Body Shop at *nos 157–159* and W H Smith at *no 152*. At the junction of Kalverstraat and Spui is the splendid Empire-style building recently given a hi-tech interior for the fashion chain, Esprit.

On Muntplein, alongside the Munttoren, is De Porceleyne Fles, the official outlet for genuine handpainted Delftware, marked on the base with the letter D, a considerably superior product to the cheap mass-produced blue and white pottery sold as Delft in many souvenir shops. A few steps away, on Singel, is the Bloemenmarkt (Flower Market), where 15 florists sell bulbs, seeds, floral bouquets, and even clipped box topiary from floating stalls. The florists can advise on customs regulations concerning the import of plant materials and will arrange shipping.

Turning left at the end of Singel brings you to Koenigsplein and Leidsestraat, another busy shopping thoroughfare. The highlight here is Metz & Co, which sells the products of top international designers – furniture,

Amsterdam shops cater for all tastes

fabrics, kitchenware, glass and smaller gift items such as ornaments and toiletries. The striking post-modernist café on the top floor is a good place to rest your feet and enjoy fine views.

*A mouthwatering
display of fine cheeses*

*Sunflowers for sale
in the Singel
flowermarket*

*Many visitors look for traditional
clogs to take home*

*Waterlooplein market is a
fascinating place to browse*

Markets

Albert Cuypstraat is the venue for Amsterdam's main market (Monday to Saturday 9am to 5pm), a crowded, colourful and vibrant affair attended by up to 50,000 people on a typical Saturday – over 7 per cent of the city's population. The stalls and milling crowds stretch for nearly a mile making this Europe's biggest general market. It occupies the heart of the district known as the 'Pijp' – the Pipe – because the long, narrow and slightly curving streets resemble the stem of an old-fashioned clay pipe. The market has a festive social air because people come here to be seen and to meet friends as much as to shop. The eye is one moment diverted by the stalls piled high with exotic fish and vegetables, colourful cheeses and bolts of fabric, the next by the passing parade of people of all the races that make up this multi-ethnic city.

Albert Cuypstraat sells useful things – clothes, food, even livestock and pets – whereas Amsterdam's other big market, on Waterlooplein (Monday to Friday 9am–5pm; Saturday 8.30am–5.30pm) is a flea market in the very real sense, but it still makes for fascinating browsing and just occasionally you might pick up an art deco vase, a mirror or some knick-knack that you cannot resist. Bargaining over the price is all part of the fun. Amsterdam has several other markets along the same lines, selling junk and near antiques – on Noordermarkt every Monday from 7.30am to 1.30pm, on Nieuwmarkt from May to September every Sunday from 10am to 5pm, and in the indoor arcade called De Looier, entered from Elandsgracht 109, open Monday to Thursday 11am to 5pm and Saturday 9am to 5pm. Less well known by visitors are the Sunday art markets on the Spui and Thorbecheplein.

Stamp and coin collectors should visit the specialist market on Nieuwezijds Voorburgwal, held every Wednesday and Saturday from 10am to 4pm, while the covered arcade of the Oudemanhuispoort is a permanent market for second-hand books (mostly in Dutch) open Monday to Saturday 10am to 4pm. Finally, all self-respecting greens and ecologists do their weekly shopping at the Boerenmarkt (Farmers' Market) on Noordermarkt (Saturday 10am to 1pm) where all the produce on sale is organic. Ironically there is another, far from ecological, market alongside; the weekly pet market.

SPECIALITY SHOPS

Characterful small shops are to be found all over Amsterdam, especially along the quiet, village-like streets of the canal circle or in chic P C Hooftstraat in the Museum Quarter. Here you are likely to find just the gift (for yourself, or for friends) that proved so elusive in the busier shopping thoroughfares. This directory is by no means exhaustive, but it does cover some of the most distinctive shops in the city.

Antiques

The Spiegelkwartier is renowned for its concentration of antique shops where you can pick up relatively inexpensive Dutch tiles or spend a fortune on an Old Master. In Nieuwe Spiegelstraat, **Kunsthandel Aalderink**, *no 15*, specialises in oriental and ethnographic art; **F G Glebbing**, *no 70*, has a good stock of furniture; **Kunsthandel Frans Leidelmeijer**, *no 58*, specialises in art deco glass, lamps, statues and ceramics; and the **Amsterdam Antiques**

Genever bottles make an attractive gift

Gallery, *no 34*, has 10 dealers under one roof, selling icons, clocks, pewter, paintings and scientific instruments amongst other things.

The prices are slightly lower in Kerkstraat where **De Haas**, *no 155*, specialises in art nouveau and art deco, and **Lambiek**, *no 78*, sells thousands of antique comics and the original drawings of comic artists and cartoonists.

Outside the Spiegelkwartier, **'t Winkeltje**, *Prinsengracht 228*, is a wonderful jumble of inexpensive antique toys, bottles, lamps, glass and candlesticks.

Books

The **English Open Book Exchange**, *Prinsengracht 42*, sells second-hand titles and will accept your unwanted books in part exchange. **Architectura et Natura**, *Leliegracht 44*, has a comprehensive stock of books in every language on architecture, wildlife and gardening and sometimes mounts exhibitions on the work of the Dutch architectural movements. **Athenaeum**, *Spui 14–16*, stocks the city's widest range of

non-fiction titles. Jacob van
Wijngaarden, *Overtoom 136*, is the best
for maps and guide books to anywhere
in the world.

Cakes and confectionery
Oldenburg, *P C Hooftstraat 97*, has
ravishing window displays and
specialises in up-market patisserie and
handmade chocolates.

Camera supplies
Foto Professional, *Nieuwendijk 113*.

Candles
Kramer, *Reestraat 20*, sells nothing but
candles from all over the world in an
extraordinary range of colours and
shapes – works of art in wax that you
will not want to set alight.

Cheese
Wegewijs Kaas, *Rozengracht 32*, proves
that there is far more to Dutch cheese
than Edam and Gouda; Kef,
Marnixstraat 192, has a superb range of
French farmhouse cheeses, and is ideal
for picnic supplies since it also sells
wine, baguettes, sausages and pâtés.

Chocolates
Hendrikse Le Confiseur, *Overtoon 448*,
makes beautiful chocolates using the
finest cocoa. While at Macrander,
Vijzelstraat 125, you can indulge in rich
cakes in the tearoom before buying
giftwrapped chocolates and marzipan
specialities.

Cigars and tobacco
P G C Hajenius, *Rokin 92–96*, is
renowned for its old-world atmosphere,
its own brand of cigars and its huge
collection of pipes.
A window for the discerning cigar smoker

Clogs
De Klompenboer, *Nieuwezijds
Voorburgwal 20*, and 't Klompenhuisje,
Nieuwe Hoogstraat 9A, both make serious
clogs that are meant to be worn, and
decorative versions for hanging on the
wall.

Clothes
Couturiers and boutiques in P C
Hooftstraat cater for the moneyed end of
the market: Edgar Vos, *no 134*, sells
beautifully tailored clothes for female
executives and the male equivalent is
Façade, *no 79*. Children with expensive
tastes are catered for at Pauw, *no 48*,
and Hobbit, *no 42*. More affordable are
shops specialising in vintage or antique
garments, such as Lady Day,
Hartenstraat 9, and Rose Rood,
Kinkerstraat 159, whose stock includes
real collector's items.

Glassware, a decorative mementoe of Amsterdam

Condoms

The Condomerie het Gulden Vlies, *Warmoestraat 141*, has a mind-boggling selection, presented with style.

Ethnic Art

Baobab, *Elandsgracht 128*, is packed with jewellery, furniture and carpets from the Far East.

Fabrics

Capsicum, *Oude Hoogstraat 1*, specialises in Thai silks and Indian cottons, whilst TIKAL Native Expression, *Hartenstraat 2A*, sells hand-dyed cottons from Guatemala, either as finished garments or by the length. Near by, McLennan's, *Hartenstraat 22*, specialises in Chinese silk.

Glass and ceramics

Focke & Meltzer, *P C Hooftstraat 65–67*, is a long-established firm selling glass, silver and ceramics from top European producers, and is a showcase for both Delftware and Royal Makkum pottery, still made according to 17th-century glazing techniques. The Galleria d'Arte 'Rinascimento' specialises in antique and reproduction Delftware and Makkum pottery and the stock ranges from thimbles to tile paintings, tulip vases and apothecaries' jars.

Greetings cards

Cards for Days, *Huidenstraat 510*, stocks humorous cards for all occasions and novelty gifts.

Herbal remedies

Jacob Hooij, *Kloveniersburgwal 12*, sells homeopathic remedies from an original apothecary's shop.

Kites

Flying Objects, *Tweede Tuindwaarstraat 8*, and Joe's de Vliegerwinkel, *Nieuwe Hoogstraat 19*, both sell ready made and do-it-yourself kites as well as boomerangs and frisbees.

A tight spot?

Lace

The genuine article, handmade rather
than machine-produced Dutch lace, can
be bought at Het Kantenhuis,
Kalverstraat 124.

Models

The Scale Train House,
Bilderdijkstraat 94, sells far more than its
name suggests: do-it-yourself
construction kits of everything from
windmills and three-masted sailing ships
to moon-landing craft, as well as a huge
stock of railway engines, track and
scenery.

Postcards and posters

All of Amsterdam's three main museums
sell first-class reproductions of the art in
their collections. Art Unlimited,
Keizersgracht 510, has an enormous stock
from around the world.

Spectacle frames

Antique and old fashioned spectacle
frames are the speciality of Donald E
Jungejans, *Noorderkerkstraat 18*,
whose stock often features in period
films, such as Bertolucci's *The Last
Emperor.*

Teeth

De Witte Tandenwinkel (The White
Teeth Shop) is an eccentric but
successful outlet for everything to do
with dental hygiene; champagne-
flavoured toothpaste and novelty tooth-
brushes are among the best-selling lines.

Tea and coffee

The products of Geels en Co,
Warmoesstraat 67, scent the whole street
and the shop is a museum of the history
of tea and coffee making and historic
packaging. Keizer, *Prinsengracht 180*,
has a vast stock and an antique tiled
interior.

Tesselschade Toys

Toys

Beautifully made toys in wood are a
Dutch speciality and many are no doubt
bought by grown-up collectors who have
no intention of allowing them to become
play worn. They can be found at
Tesselschade, *Leidseplein 33*, the Bell
Tree, *Spiegelgracht 10*, De Speelmuis,
Elandsgracht 5 and, in the same street at
no 116, Annabelle.

Videos

Cine-Qua-Non, *Staalstraat 14*, is a film-
lovers' haven, stocking videotapes of cult
and art movies that are not widely
available on the commercial market, as
well as all kinds of posters, magazines,
books and memorabilia to do with
cinema.

Diamonds

Amsterdam has been an important centre for diamond processing since the 17th century. The industry was founded by Jewish refugees who were prohibited from joining the well-established city guilds, which effectively barred them from many areas of employment. They therefore pursued trades which were not regulated – retail trading, banking, printing and diamond working. From these roots the industry blossomed, partly due to the skill of Amsterdam's diamond cutters and polishers, and partly because the Dutch colonies in South Africa proved to be a rich source of raw diamonds. This led to a boom during the so-called Kaapse Tijd (Cape Age) of the 1870s when diamond processing became the city's fastest growing sector.

Today Amsterdam's diamond companies concentrate on the jewellery trade since artificial diamonds, invented in the 1950s, are now used for most industrial applications.

Several companies offer workshop tours where visitors may learn how rough diamonds are turned into sparkling gems. You will discover the factors that influence the price. These are the four Cs of the diamond trade: the colour (diamonds can be green, blue, rose, yellow and brown as well as pure white), the cut (the number of facets), the clarity (dictated by the number and size of inclusions) and the carat (the weight; 1 carat = 0.2gms). Visitors are also sure to be told about the world's biggest diamond, the Cullinan (found in South Africa, 1905), which weighed 3,106 carats in its rough state; it was cut into 105 separate gems of which the largest, Cullinan I (530 carats), the world's largest cut diamond, is now the central jewel in the British crown.

The following diamond companies all give tours on request, lasting from 30 minutes to an hour:

Amsterdam Diamond Centre, *Rokin 1–5 (tel: 624 5787); tours take place Monday to Wednesday, Friday and Saturday 10am– 5.30pm, Thursday 10am–8.30pm and Sunday 10.30am–5.30pm.*

Van Moppes Diamonds, *Albert Cuypstraat 2–6 (tel: 676 1242), open daily in summer 8.30am– 6.30pm, closed Sunday in winter.*

Coster Diamonds, *Paulus Potterstraat 2–6 (tel: 676 2222), open Monday to Saturday 9am– 5pm, Sunday 10am–5pm.*

Gassan Diamond House, *Nieuwe Uilenburgerstraat 173–175 (tel: 622 5333), open Monday to Friday 9am–5.30pm.*

Diamonds can be anyone's best friend in Amsterdam. Business is booming, though not everyone will want to take a souvenir home

Entertainment

*A*msterdam's lively entertainment scene caters to every taste; it is estimated that over 14,000 concerts or theatrical performances take place in the city every year – an average of 40 a day. The VVV Tourist Information Centre publishes a useful fortnightly listings magazine, *What's on in Amsterdam,* which specifically concentrates on events that can be enjoyed by English-speaking visitors.

CLASSICAL MUSIC, BALLET AND OPERA
Muziektheater
The Muziektheater is part of the controversial modern Stopera development (see Stadhuis in the **What to See** section) and it is dogged by poor acoustics; this makes performances by the Netherlands Opera less than perfect, but the problem has been overcome to a degree by the strategic use of hidden microphones. The Dutch National Ballet is also based here and its performances of classics, such as *Swan Lake* and *Sleeping Beauty* play to capacity audiences, so advance booking is advisable. The Netherlands Dance Theatre puts in occasional guest performances of modern choreography. Musicians from the opera and ballet orchestras give free lunchtime concerts in summer.
Waterlooplein 22 (tel: 625 5455)
Box office open: Monday to Saturday

Concertgebouw

The controversial Muziektheater development

10am–6pm; Sunday 12 noon–6pm
Tram 9, 14 or Waterlooplein Metro

Concertgebouw

By contrast with the Muziektheater, the Concertgebouw is renowned for its acoustics which are exploited to the full by the Royal Concertgebouw Orchestra, internationally famous for performances of the big rich works of Mahler, Strauss, Ravel and Debussy. Under its Milan-born chief conductor, Riccardo Chailly, the repertoire has expanded to include 20th-century music and new work. Concerts are very well supported so advance booking is advisable.

Concertgebouwplein 2–6 (tel: 671 8345)
Box office open: Monday to Saturday 10am–5pm
Trams 3, 5, 12 or 16.

Beurs van Berlage

Amsterdam's former stock and commodities exchange is now a cultural centre, home to The Netherlands Philharmonic and Chamber Orchestras who perform in two superbly converted halls named after their commercial sponsors, the AGA Zaal and the Wang Zaal. Concerts cover the whole musical repertoire and occasionally feature top international soloists.

Damrak 213 (tel: 627 0466)
Box office open: Tuesday to Saturday 12.30pm–6pm
Trams 4, 9, 16, 24 or 25

Churches

The Engelsekerk *(Begijnhof 48)* hosts free lunchtime concerts in July and August and a full programme of evening concerts throughout the year. Look out for occasional organ recitals and choral concerts in Oude Kerk and Nieuwe Kerk. The Waalsekerk *(Oudezijds Achterburgwal)* is used for early music recitals and the Ronde Lutherse Kerk *(Kattengat 1)* hosts popular 'Coffee Time' concerts at 11am every Sunday.

IJsbreker

This small concert hall-cum-café and exhibition centre has built a Europe-wide reputation for its stimulating programme of new works.

Weesperzijde 23 (tel: 668 1805)
Box office open: Monday to Friday 9am–5.30pm
Tram 3, 6, 7, 10 or Weesperplein Metro

JAZZ
BIMHuis

The city's main jazz venue, located in a converted warehouse, was founded in 1974 by BIM, the jazz musicians' union, and ever since it has been attracting the best of the world's performers across the spectrum – from trad to avant-garde. The atmosphere is relaxed and the audience hugely appreciative. Concerts are given three nights a week, on Thursday, Friday and Saturday, and there are often free jam sessions in the café on other nights.

Oudeschans 73 (tel: 623 3373)
Box office open: Thursday to Saturday
8pm–9pm (ie one hour before the
performance starts). Tickets can also be
booked for that night's concert only at the
VVV Tourist Information Centre
Tram 9, 14 or Nieuwemarkt Metro

Joseph Lam's Dixieland Jazz Club

Another warehouse venue, this time in the western docks area, that is packed every Saturday and Sunday night with fans of traditional and Dixieland jazz.

Van Diemenstraat 242 (tel: 622 8086)
Tickets on sale at the door (no advance
booking); concerts Saturday and Sunday
from 9pm. Tram 3

Getting ready to rock in Dam square

ROCK MUSIC
Melkweg

Milky Way – located in an old dairy – was the last bastion of hippiedom until the late 1970s when the building was converted to a modern multi-media centre with a theatre, cinema, and concert hall, the latter specialising in world music, reggae, African, South American and roots music, but also playing host to well-known British and American bands.

Melkweg is run as a co-operative and is informal and relaxed; there is no dress code, but regulars do turn up in imaginative party dress, especially for the popular Friday and Saturday night discos.

Lijnbaansgracht 234A (tel: 624 1777)
Open: Tuesday to Sunday from 7.30pm;
disco Friday and Saturday after the live
acts, around 1am.
Trams 1, 2, 5, 6, 7 or 10

Paradiso

This rock venue, converted from a redundant church, offers concerts from big-name bands who love the informal atmosphere and intimacy as a change from the impersonality of huge sports stadium venues. Like its near neighbour Melkweg, world music, reggae, African and Latin music all feature strongly.

Weteringschans 6–8 (tel: 624 4521)
Concerts from 8pm on various days; phone
for details; tickets at the door or from the
VVV Tourist Information Centre
Trams 6, 7 or 10

Maloe Melo

This dark, smoky and rather cramped bar is highly regarded for its rhythm and blues acts; admission is free and the atmosphere friendly.

Lijnbaansgracht 160 (tel: 625 3300)
Open: Monday to Friday from 10pm
Trams 10, 13, 14 or 17

CINEMA

Almost all films are shown in their original language versions (predominantly English) or with English subtitles; the few exceptions that are only shown in Dutch will feature the words *Nederlands Gesproken* on the poster. Several cinemas mount special afternoon matinees featuring cartoons, science fiction or children's films. Cinema listings are found in numerous bars and cafés as well as in *What's On in Amsterdam* and in the free monthly magazine *De Filmkrant* (in Dutch but easily understood).

Calypso/Bellevue Cinerama
Glitzy two-screen cinema showing the latest popular movies.
Marnixstraat 400 (tel: 623 4876)
Trams 7 or 10

City
The biggest cinema in Amsterdam with seven screens; expect to queue at weekends for popular blockbuster movies.
Leidseplein (tel: 623 4579)
Trams 1, 2, 5, 6, 7 or 10

The magnificent art deco façade of the Tuschinski cinema

Tuschinski
Worth visiting just for its beautiful and authentic 1920s interior; Amsterdam's showcase cinema used for celebrity premières. Expect queues at weekends if you have not booked in advance.
Reguliersbreestraat 26 (tel: 626 2633)
Box office open: daily 12.15pm–10pm
Trams 9 or 14

The Movies
Excellent neighbourhood cinema specialising in international art movies and classics with an authentic 1930s café.
Haarlemmerdijk 161 (tel: 624 5790)
Tram 3

Nederlands Filmmuseum
The films shown here are drawn from the museum's archives, everything from silent movies (shown with live piano accompaniment) to the art films of Truffaut and Tarkovsky – the whole gamut of European cinema, in fact, and with three different films a day there is plenty of choice. In summer, the terrace of this 19th-century former tea room is used for outdoor screenings.
Vondelpark 3 (tel 683 1646)
Box office open daily from 8.30am
Trams 1, 2, 3, 5, 6 or 12

THEATRE
Stadsschouwburg
The Municipal Theatre is largely devoted to the classics; *Gijsbrecht van Aemstel*, a historical drama written in 1638 by Joost van den Vandel, the Shakespeare of The Netherlands, is regularly performed, but only in Dutch. On the other hand, you will also find English-language productions of Shakespeare, Shaw, Brecht, Ibsen and Chekhov given by visiting British and American companies or by the city's own ESTA – the English Speaking

The Municipal Theatre by night

Theatre of Amsterdam.
Leidseplein 26 (tel: 624 2311)
Box office open: Monday to Saturday
10am–6pm
Trams 1, 2, 5, 6, 7 or 10
De Stalhouderij
The 'Livery Stable' is an intimate theatre run by an international artists' collective specialising in contemporary English-language plays, renowned for the high quality of their performances; productions are popular so book in advance.
1e Bloemdwarsstraat 4 (tel: 626 2282)
Telephone bookings: Monday to Saturday
12 noon–5pm
Box office open: 8pm–8.30pm (ie just before the start of performances)
Trams 13 or 17
Theater Carré
This former circus building is now the venue for big musical and theatrical productions touring from Britain and the USA – *Cats*, *Sweet Charity* and *Les Misérables* were among the recent shows.
Amstel 111–125 (tel: 622 5825)
Box office open: Monday to Saturday
10am–7pm, Sunday 1pm–2pm
Trams 6, 7 or 10

OPEN-AIR EVENTS
On summer Sunday afternoons it can seem that everyone in Amsterdam is heading for Vondelpark; the open-air theatre here is used for a very broad range of concerts, from traditional jazz to brass band music and even rock performances by home-grown bands such as The Nits. Between stage acts, there are buskers, jugglers, acrobats and puppeteers to watch. Check what is on at the VVV Tourist Information Centre or just turn up and take pot luck.
Vondelpark: entrance from PC Hooftstraat
Trams 1, 2, 3, 5, 6 or 12

The breathtaking interior of the Tuschinski cinema

Colourful modern art in the form of street grafitti decorates a small corner of Vondelpark, a green area renowned for its open-air theatre

FESTIVALS

The people of Amsterdam are always ready to take to the streets and join in the spontaneous fun that surrounds their numerous festivals. Visitors are welcome to join in, flowing with the crowd.

January: New Year is seen in with fireworks and firecrackers, a symbolic way of scaring off the devils and ghosts of dreary winter. Revellers sustain themselves by consuming quantities of *olie bollen* (doughnuts) plus bottles of champagne; the big squares, such as Nieuwmarkt, Leidseplein, Rembrandtsplein and Dam square, see most of the action and street performers of every kind take their turn at entertaining the crowds.

February/March: If the weather turns cold enough to freeze the canals and waterways, an event that occurs only once in every 10 years or so, everyone brings out their skates. In the northern Netherlands the big event, weather

Queen's Day celebrations

permitting, is the *Elfstedentocht,* the 11-towns race, a real test of skaters' skill and stamina, which Amsterdammers keenly follow on television.

April: 30 April is Koninginnedag (Queen's Day), the Queen's official birthday (her real birthday is on 31 January). Once this was a festival for children, who would set up stalls selling their handmade sweets and cakes or unwanted toys, to earn some pocket money, but today everyone joins in, setting up stalls in front of their homes so that Amsterdam turns into a huge street market. Buskers and street performers add to the fun and many bars set up outdoor stages where jazz, folk and rock bands entertain the customers. Leidseplein and Vondelpark are the best places to savour the atmosphere.

June: The month-long Holland Festival is a prestigious showcase for the arts – dance, ballet, theatre, music and opera. Top performers from all over the world take part (programme information from Holland Festival, *Kleine*

*Gartmanplantsoen 21, 1017 RP
Amsterdam; tel: 627 6566).*

On the second Sunday in June the streets of the canal circle are closed to traffic for the Echo Grachtenloop marathon.

July: The 10-day Zomerfestijn (Summer Festival) is the fringe equivalent to the highbrow Holland Festival. The whole spectrum of progressive art is represented, from electronic music, video and light shows to mime, dance and experimental theatre, much of it performed in the open air. Information and tickets, during the festival only, from Grand Café Dulac, *Haarlemmerstraat 118 (tel: 627 4394).*

August: One of the most enjoyable events of the year is the free Prinsengracht classical concert held one evening in the last week of August; this usually features a top international pianist who performs from a floating platform in front of the Pulitzer Hotel *(Prinsengracht 315–331).* Appreciative music-lovers come with picnics and champagne to line the canal banks (information from the Cristofori piano shop, *Prinsengracht 579, tel: 626 8485).*

At the end of the month, the Museum Quarter hosts the Uitmarkt, a huge cultural fair at which arts companies from all over The Netherlands perform extracts from their forthcoming season's programme in order to help ticket sales.

September: The Bloemen Corso (Flower Parade), held on the first Saturday in September, is a spectacular affair organised by florists and horticulturalists; their huge and decorative floats, smothered in flowers,

The Flower Parade takes to the streets

are driven from the flower auction at Aalsmeer through the streets of Amsterdam to a reception in Dam Square.

National Monument Day, on the second Saturday in September, provides an opportunity to see inside some of Amsterdam's finest protected monuments, including private homes and office premises in the canal circle.

The Jordaan Festival, in the second and third week of September, is a riotous fortnight of music, fancy dress and beer consumption in which the Jordaan district extends a friendly welcome to all comers.

November/December: St Nicolaas, the Dutch equivalent of Santa Claus arrives in Amsterdam on the third Saturday in November (around the 17th), landing by steamboat 'from Spain' at Centraal station and parading up Damrak, distributing sweets to crowds of wide-eyed children. Dutch children traditionally receive their presents on the feast of St Nicolaas (5 December), although increasingly they are indulged with a second round of presents on 25 December as well.

Children

Amsterdam is a perfect city for children, who will enjoy canal trips, barrel organs, street buskers and riding the trams as much, if not more, than their parents. Most museums charge lower admission fees for children and admit infants for free.

Favourite children's attractions in the city are **Madame Tussaud Scenerama** and the **Spaarpotten** (Money Box) Museum. Two museums are specifically aimed at children: the **Kindermuseum TM Junior** allows them to learn about life in Bali, Peru or Senegal through imaginative reconstructions of streets and houses and organised music, dance, cooking and storytelling activities. The

Children at play

Technisch Museum is full of push-button models that explain the wonders of holography, lasers, optical illusions, computers and cars. The big attraction for children at the **Scheepvaart** (Maritime) Museum is the **East Indiaman** moored in the dock whose narrow passages, staircases and hold can be explored without restriction. The Aviodome at Schiphol airport provides the opportunity to play at being pilot in the cockpit of an airliner or to examine a space capsule at close quarters.

The zoo (Artis) is an absorbing place because it combines so many attractions: there is a planetarium and an aquarium to explore as well as a big collection of wild animals and a smaller corner, set up as a children's farm, where the rabbits and goats can be touched and stroked.

Amsterdam has several other children's farms which are not so crowded and which cost nothing to visit (though donations are welcomed). The farm in the Pijp district, **De Dierenpijp** (Lizzy Ansinghstraat), can be combined with a visit to the nearby **Technisch Museum** *(tel: 664 8303; open Monday and Wednesday to Sunday 1pm–5pm; tram 12 or 25)*. At the junction of Bickersgracht and Zandhoek, in the Western Islands (see **Unknown Amsterdam**), the **Kinderboerderij Om de Hoek**, the Children's Farm on the Corner, is open during daylight hours; children can help with the feeding if they are there at the right time – usually around 4pm.

PARKS AND PLAYGROUNDS
Vondelpark is the most central of

Amsterdam's green spaces; apart from the playground and the numerous ducks on the lake, there is plenty of free entertainment on summer weekends – acrobats, puppeteers and musicians. **Amsterdamse Bos** can form the focus of a whole day's outing, beginning and ending with a ride on a veteran tram from the **Electrische Tramlijn Museum**; the options here include cycling, swimming, boating, horse riding and playground facilities.

SWIMMING

The **Mirandabad complex** is a great place for burning up energy; the indoor sub-tropical pool has water slides, a wave machine and whirlpool and there is an outdoor pool as well for summer use.
De Mirandalaan 9
(tel: 642 8080/644 6637)
Open: Monday 7am–10.15pm; Tuesday 12.15pm–10.15 pm; Wednesday 7am–5.30pm; Thursday 7pm–10.15pm; Friday 7am–10.15pm; Saturday and Sunday 10am–5.30pm
Admission charge
Tram 25 or bus 8, 48, 60 and 158.

CINEMA

Several cinemas in Amsterdam have special children's matinees – check with individual cinemas for details.

THEATRE

The Kindertheater Elleboog may appeal to older children; this is a club which trains children in circus techniques – conjuring, clowning, juggling, unicycle riding and so on – but there are open sessions for all comers on Saturday afternoons and all day Sunday, and the staff speak English. It is essential to book places for your children in advance.
Passeerdersgracht 32 (tel: 626 9370)
Admission charge
Tram 7 or 10.

BABYSITTERS

Oppascentrale Kriterion is a thoroughly reliable agency employing students who charge very modest rates – hence it is essential to book in advance, especially for weekends *(tel: 624 5848)*.

A healthy combination of fun and learning at the Artis Natura

Sports

Participant

*A*msterdammers are not great sports fanatics or fitness freaks, but there are numerous opportunities for working out or taking a relaxing sauna in the city centre.

HEALTH CLUBS
Splash
An up-market fitness centre which has a weights room, exercise gym, Turkish bath, sauna and massage service as well as aerobics classes throughout the day.
Looiersgracht 26 (tel: 624 8404)
Open: Monday to Friday 10am–10pm;
Saturday and Sunday 11am–6pm
Admission charge: a day pass allows free use of all the facilities
Trams 7 or 10.

A universal sight, this time in Vondelpark

Sporting Club Leidseplein
Luxurious and central establishment with exercise gymnasium and sauna; aerobics classes for all levels of fitness take place on Monday, Wednesday and Friday at 7pm.
Korte Leidsedwarsstraat 18 (tel: 620 6631)
Open: Monday to Friday 9am–midnight;
Saturday and Sunday 10am–6pm
Admission charge: a day pass allows free use of all facilities
Trams 1, 2, 5, 6, 7 or 10.

SPORTS CENTRES
Borchland
Squash, tennis and badminton courts and indoor bowling green under one roof.
Borchlandweg 8–12 (tel: 696 1441)
Open: daily 7.30am–midnight
Admission charge: courts should be booked in advance; higher rates evenings and weekends
Bus 169.

SQUASH
Dickysquash
Facilities include a sauna and exercise room.
Ketelmarkerstraat 6 (tel: 626 7883)
Open: Monday to Friday
8.45am–11.15pm; Saturday and Sunday
8.45pm–9pm
Admission charge: higher rates evenings and Sunday.

Aquatic fun at the Mirandabad

SWIMMING
Marnixbad
Indoor 25m pool with water slides, whirlpool and sauna, centrally located.
Marnixstraat 5–9 (tel: 625 4843)
Open: Monday 7am–9am, 12 noon–
1.30pm, 3pm–5pm; Tuesday and
Wednesday 7am–5.30pm; Thursday 7am–
10am, 11am–5pm; Friday 7am–10am,
11am–5.30pm; Saturday 10am–12 noon;
Sunday 3.30pm–5.30pm
Admission charge
Trams 3, 7, 10 or bus 18.

Mirandabad
Popular, clean sub-tropical pool with wave machine, beach, water slide, whirlpool and outdoor pool in summer.
De Mirandalaan 9
(tel: 642 8080/644 6637)
Open: Monday 7am–10.15pm; Tuesday
12.15pm–10.15 pm; Wednesday 7am–
5.30pm; Thursday 7pm–10.15pm; Friday
7am–10.15pm; Saturday and Sunday
10am–5.30pm
Admission charge
Tram 25 or bus 8, 48, 60 and 158.

Zuiderbad
Indoor pool built in 1912 and retaining its tiled period interior.
Hobbemastraat 26 (tel: 679 2217)
Open: Monday 7am–6pm, 7pm–10.30pm;
Tuesday 7am–9am, 12 noon–5pm, 6pm–
9.30pm; Wednesday 7am–10am, 12 noon–
10.30pm; Thursday 7am–9.30am, 12
noon–6pm; Friday 7am–9pm; Saturday
8am–5pm; Sunday 10am–3.30pm
Admission charge
Trams 1, 2, 5, 16, 24 or 25.

TENNIS ´
Amstelpark
Ten indoor and 16 outdoor courts; free racket hire.
Karel Lotsylaan 8 (tel: 644 5436)
Open: daily 8am–midnight. Hourly court fee
Buses 26, 48, 65, 148, 158 or 197.

WATERSPORTS
Sloterpark
Watersports centre on the Sloterplas lake with dinghies, windsurfing boards, canoes and wetsuits for hire.
Noordzijde 41 (tel: 613 8855)
Open: May to October, Monday to Friday
9am–6pm, Saturday and Sunday
11am–5pm
Hourly hire charge; deposit required, take
your passport as evidence of identity
Bus 19 or 47.

Outdoor tennis in Vondelpark

Sports

Spectator

*M*ost of the big sporting events take place outside Amsterdam but the venues are easily reached by public transport or by joining a special coach excursion.

EQUESTRIAN SPORTS

Paardendag, a two-day equestrian event, takes place in Den Haag (The Hague) in the second week in June *(details from The Hague VVV Tourist Information Centre, tel: 070 354 6200)*. Rotterdam hosts the biggest horse show of the year in mid-August *(details from the Rotterdam VVV Tourist Information Centre, tel 010 413 6000)*. Amsterdam's own RAI exhibition centre is the venue for **The Netherlands International Horse Show** in the first week of November *(details from the Amsterdam VVV Tourist Information Centre, tel: 020 626 6444)*.

Mighty Ajax take on Gromingen

FOOTBALL

Ajax, Amsterdam's home team, reached the peak of its success in the 1970s when it won three European Cup tournaments. Disgrace followed when the team was banned from European competition for a year because of the violent behaviour of its fans, and this was followed by a scandal involving underhand transfer deals.

Under new management the team has experienced a renaissance and won the Dutch championship in 1990. The fans are better behaved but matches against old rivals such as Feyenoord of Rotterdam, FC Den Haag, FC Utrecht and PSV Eindhoven are heavily policed as a precautionary measure. Trouble can

be avoided by buying seat tickets and avoiding the standing areas of the ground.
Middenweg 401 (tel: 694 6515)
Matches: June to September, Sunday 2.30pm
Admission charge
Tram 9 or buses 138, 150, 152, 154, 158.

GOLF
The KLM Open Championship takes place at the beach resort of Zandvoort, west of Amsterdam, at the end of July.
Details from The Nederlands Golf Federatie (tel: 035 830 565).

HOCKEY
The Wagener Stadium in Amsterdam is the home ground of the city's own highly regarded men's and women's teams and it is also used to stage international competitions.
Nieuwe Kalfjslaan (tel: 640 1141)
Matches: September to May, Sunday
Women 12.45pm, Men 2.30pm
Admission free to league games, admission charge for internationals
Buses 125, 170, 171, 172, 173 or 194.

MOTOR SPORTS
The Zaandvoort Circuit, a short train ride from Amsterdam, is no longer used for Formula 1 racing but there is an exciting choice of international events held every weekend from March to October; details from Esso garages or t*el: 02507 18284.*

The big event of the year is the International Netherlands Motorcycling **TT Grand Prix** held at Assen at the end of June. This popular event includes vintage, Formula 1 and sidecar races. Advance booking by post advised.
TT Assen, PO Box 150, 9400 AD Assen.
For general information tel: 05920 55000.

Grand Prix racing at Zaandvoort

TENNIS
The International Tennis Tournament, held in Rotterdam at the end of February and beginning of March, provides an opportunity to see some of the world's top-seeded players in action.
Information from the Rotterdam VVV Tourist Information Centre (tel: 010 413 6000).

WINDSURFING
The challenging conditions of the North Sea make the International Windsurfing Event, held in mid-October at Scheveningen, just outside Den Haag, a spectacular event.
Details from The Hague VVV Tourist Information Centre (tel: 070 354 6200).

Food and Drink

Night life in Amsterdam caters to every taste

It is said that you can eat the food of every nation somewhere in Amsterdam, from American and Argentinian to Swiss, Thai or Turkish. The claim is well founded since Amsterdam has hundreds of good restaurants serving every kind of cuisine imaginable, including some that you may never have tried, such as Surinamese. In addition there are several gourmet shrines - top restaurants that have won Europe-wide acclaim for their inventiveness and quality, most of them French inspired. These are inevitably expensive, but the majority of the city's restaurants are informal, inexpensive and geared to ordinary wallets.

Amsterdammers themselves do not like pretentiousness in any form and want to relax when they eat out. Restaurateurs have to fit in to survive, hence you will find that children are

welcome in most restaurants and that there is nearly always a good vegetarian selection on the menu. Only the most expensive restaurants insist on jacket and tie, otherwise people dress as casually as they please. Neither is there pressure on diners to buy an expensive bottle of wine – most local people prefer a cooling beer or mineral water instead. Another aspect of the easy-going attitude is that few restaurants have smoke-free areas, though the air-conditioning usually takes care of the problem.

There should be no difficulty understanding the menus, which are printed in several languages; waiters will speak English, and often French and German as well. The menu prices include tax (18.5 per cent) and service (15 per cent) so there is no need to worry about hidden extras. Tips are not expected but you will generally receive such good service that you will be happy to leave some small change for the waiter. Credit cards are universally accepted.

A number of the restaurants listed below are quite small, so it is advisable to book in advance for dinner, especially in summer and at weekends.

The following price indications are based on the cost of a full meal (starter, main course and dessert) per person, but do not include the price of drinks:

F under F35
FF F35 to F45
FFF F45 to F75
FFFF F75 and above

AMERICAN
The American Place FF
The place to go if you cannot survive without authentic American hamburgers, served big and juicy with all the trimmings. Good steaks and cajun food as well.
Utrechtsedwarstraat 141 (tel: 620 7893)
Open: Thursday to Monday 5pm–11.30pm
Tram 4.

ARGENTINIAN
Tango Grill Restaurant FF
Family-run restaurant serving succulent charcoal-grilled steaks to the backround of tango music; try *budin de pan,* Argentinian bread pudding, as an unusual but enjoyable dessert.
Warmoesstraat 49 (tel: 627 2467)
Open: daily 5pm–midnight
Trams 4, 9, 16, 24 or 25.

CAJUN
Cajun Louisiana FF
Clam chowder and catfish cooked in black butter, plus vegetarian specialities.
Ceinturbaan 260 (tel: 664 4729)
Open: daily 5pm–11pm
Tram 3

CARIBBEAN
Rum Runners F
Young, fun café with tropical decor renowned for its cocktails; in summer the tables spill out into the garden alongside Westerkerk. Spicy fish stews and cooling salads plus vegetarian options; other dishes seem less distinctively Caribbean and more Tex-Mex in style. Live music on Wednesday to Sunday afternoons.
Prinsengracht 277 (tel: 627 4079)
Open: Monday to Friday 4pm–1am;
Saturday and Sunday 12 noon–1am
Trams 13, 14 or 17.

An Argentine restaurant offers its national cuisine

Dutch Food and Drink

Dutch food at its best means, primarily, absolutely fresh fish and seafood served very simply. At its worst it means heavy, calorie-laden food.

The watery landscape of The Netherlands produces fresh and saltwater fish in abundance: prized mussels and oysters from the province of Zeeland, eels from the IJsselmeer, herrings and flatfish from the North Sea. The place to eat fish is **Lucius FF** *(Spuistraat 247 tel: 624 1831, open daily 5.30pm–11pm; tram 1, 2, 5, 13, 14 or 17)*. This old-fashioned establishment, with its white-tiled walls and tanks full of fish (not for eating) serves whatever is freshest and in season. The menu is chalked on a blackboard and the ambience is simple; try the *plateau de fruits de mer* for an attractively presented feast of seafood. Two other atmospheric and popular fish restaurants are **Le Pêcheur FF** *(Reguliersdwarsstraat 32, tel: 624 3121; open Monday to Friday noon to midnight Saturday and Sunday 5pm to midnight; tram 4, 9 or 14)* and **Sluizer F** *(Utrechtsestraat 45, tel: 626 3557; open same hours as Le Pêcheur; tram 4)*.

If you want to try authentic food, in all its stolidity, head for the

Hotel Port van Cleve FF *(Nieuwezijds Voorburgwal 178–180, tel: 624 4860; open 12 noon–10pm daily; tram 1, 2, 4, 9, 24, 25 or 26)*. This venerable institution has two restaurants; the slightly more expensive Blauwe Parade is renowned for its interior, covered in old Delftware picture tiles, but for traditional Dutch food you should go to the cheaper Blauwe Poort. Specialites include split pea soup, *(erwtensoep)* flavoured with bacon, and *hutspot*, a beef and vegetable dish dating back to the Spanish occupation of The Netherlands in the the mid-16th century. If these do not appeal you can also enjoy steak in both restaurants; millions have been served since the hotel opened its doors in 1870 and every 1,000th steak comes with a complimentary bottle of wine.

For day to day Dutch specialities you do not have to eat formally. Fishmongers *(vishandel)* and herring stalls *(harringkarren)* sell tempting lunchtime snacks such as marinated herring, smoked eel, prawns or fresh salmon served in a bread roll. The traditional dish is raw fresh herring, best when the mild-tasting young fish *(nieuwe harring)* is available in spring.

*e herring stall is the Amsterdammers'
dog stand*

*uthentic Dutch food is
illing as well as tasty*

*Hoogstraat: a
warning, perhaps, to
indulge in moderation*

Cafés and sandwich shops
(broodjeszaken) sell a tempting array
of filled rolls, or open sandwiches
stuffed with cheese, salami, salad
and topped with fried eggs
(uitsmijters). Equally Dutch are the
fried food stalls (frietkramen) selling
delicious chips with mayonnaise or
spicy mincemeat balls called
frikadellen.

When it comes to alcohol,
Amsterdammers have a habit of
combining their two national drinks
– pilsner-style beer and juniper
flavoured gin. The beer is drunk as
a chaser to the gin, a combination
aptly known as a kopstoot, a
headbanger. Try gin on its own just
for the experience; jonge jenever,
young gin, is an aromatic drink
often combined with a mixer such
as Coca-Cola. Such treatment
would be sacrilegious, however, to
oude jenever, old gin; this mellow,
slightly sweet and creamy liquor,
sipped ice cold from a traditional
stumpy glass, has its own distinctive
and highly addictive flavour.

Restaurants

CHINESE
Dynasty FF
Very smart and fashionable, with a modern oriental decor of parasols, potted plants, silks and orchids. The food is highly original, based on the Cantonese tradition but combining elements of Thai, Vietnamese and Indonesian cuisine.
Reguliersdwarsstraat 30 (tel: 626 8400)
Open: Wednesday to Monday 6pm–midnight. Trams 4, 9 or 1

The famed Sea Palace restaurant

Sea Palace FFF
This floating restaurant, moored in the northern docks, is popular as much for its riverside views and ambience as for its food. Excellent *dim sum* lunches are served from noon to 3.30pm and the most popular dinner dish is Peking Duck.
Oosterdokskade 8 (tel: 626 4777)
Open: daily 12 noon–10.30pm
Buses 22, 44 or 47

Treasure FFF
In general, Amsterdam Chinese restaurants offering a range of cuisines are to be avoided on the principle that the Jack of all trades is master of none; this luxurious restaurant is an exception, however, employing specialist master chefs for each of its regional cuisines – Cantonese, Peking and Szechuan – and serving excellent lunchtime *dim sum*.
Nieuwezijds Voorburgwal 115 (tel: 623 4061)
Open: daily 12 noon–3pm and 5pm–10.30pm
Trams 1, 2, 5, 13 or 17

FRENCH
Ciel Bleu FFFF
Outstanding views from the hotel's 23rd-floor restaurant complemented by top-flight nouvelle cuisine; try the *menu prestige* for a romantic special occasion.
Okura Hotel, Ferdinand Bolstraat 333 (tel: 678 7111)
Open: daily 6pm–11pm; jacket and tie
Tram 12

Excelsior FFFF
Elegant mirrored and chandeliered, Michelin-starred restaurant with panoramic views over the River Amstel. Seafood and game specialities and a comprehensive wine list.
Hotel de l'Europe, Nieuwe Doelenstraat 2–8 (tel: 623 4836)
Open: Sunday to Friday 12.30pm–2.30pm and daily 7pm–10.30pm; booking essential; jacket and tie
Trams 4, 9, 14, 16, 24 or 25

Dikker en Thijs FFFF
Long-established restaurant founded in 1915 by an Escoffier-trained chef and his grocer partner, still serving classic French haute cuisine. Similar dishes can be enjoyed in the less expensive brasserie on the ground floor which is open for lunch.
Prinsengracht 444 (tel: 625 8876/626 7721)
Open: Monday to Saturday 7pm–10pm

De Gouden Reael FFF
Former café in the characterful Western Islands (see **Unknown Amsterdam**) specialising in regional French cuisine, served with friendliness and flair. Inexpensive set menus.
Zandhoek 14 (tel: 623 3883)
Open: Monday to Friday 12 noon–2pm, daily 6pm–10pm. Tram 3

De Graaf FFFF
Michelin-starred restaurant renowned for inventiveness and a menu that changes with the seasons.
Emmalaan 25 (tel: 662 4884)
Open: Monday to Saturday 12 noon–2pm and 6pm–10pm. Tram 2

De Kersentuin FFFF
The 'Cherry Orchard' is one of the most prestigious restaurants in The Netherlands, famed for the imaginative dishes of Jon Sistermans who combines oriental flavours and presentational flair with traditional ingredients.
Garden Hotel, Dijsselhofplantsoen 7 (tel: 664 2121)
Open: Monday to Friday 12 noon–2.30pm, Monday to Saturday 6pm–10.15pm; booking essential; jacket and tie. Tram 16

Molen 'de Dikkert' FFFF
A beautiful old windmill, dating from 1672 and located in the southern suburbs, forms the unusual and surprisingly stylish setting in which to enjoy classic French cuisine.
Amsterdamseweg 104A (tel: 641 1378)
Open: Monday to Saturday 12 noon–2pm and 6pm–10pm; booking essential; jacket and tie. Bus 175

't Swarte Schaep FFF
Alone in a sea of fast-food outlets, the 'Black Sheep' maintains the highest culinary standards while remaining relatively inexpensive. Even members of the Dutch royal family come here for the subtle blend of traditional French and

Dutch cuisine, and for the characterful timbered interior of the 300-year-old building.
Korte Leidsedwarsstraat 24 (tel: 622 3021)
Open: daily 12 noon–11pm; booking advised. Trams 1, 2 or 5

Tout Court FFF
Intimate restaurant with a slightly bohemian atmosphere and clientele, patronised by artists and media personalities. Nouvelle cuisine and good value set menus. Wine only with meals.
Runstraat 13 (tel: 625 8637)
Open: Tuesday to Saturday 6pm–11.30pm; booking essential. Tram 7 or 10

De Trechter FFFF
With only eight tables, intimacy and attentive service are guaranteed in this friendly restaurant renowned for top-quality nouvelle cuisine; surprise is the key note of a chef who likes to introduce appetising extras – *amuse geueles* – at unexpected moments in the meal.
Hobbemakade 63 (tel: 671 1263)
Open: Tuesday to Saturday 6pm–11.30pm; booking essential. Tram 16

'd Vijf Vlieghen FFF
The Five Flies is rather dismissively described by Amsterdammers as a tourist trap but do not be deterred; the cooking is a blend of Dutch and French but the ambience is the main attraction – tables are set in intimate corners of a rambling old house full of period furniture and antiques, lit by candles to create an unusual and romantic atmosphere.
Spuistraat 294 (tel: 624 5214)
Open: daily 6pm–11.30pm. Tram 3

Irresistible fruit pastries

Chinese cuisine is well represented

GREEK
Aphrodite F
Inexpensive, friendly and authentic. Try the *mezes*, a multi-course set menu for a real feast.
Lange Liedsedwarsstraat 91
(tel: 622 7382)
Open: daily 5pm–midnight
Trams 1, 2, 5, 6, 7 or 10
Filoxenia F
Another small and friendly restaurant serving succulent herb-flavoured kebabs at reasonable prices.
Berenstraat 8 (tel: 624 4292)
Open: daily 6pm–midnight
Trams 1, 2 or 5

INDIAN
Koh-I-Noor FF
Popular restaurant serving all the classic northern Indian dishes plus inexpensive meat and vegetarian *thali* set menus. (Also at Rokin 18, tel: 627 2118.)
Westermarkt 29 (tel: 623 3133)
Open: daily 5pm–11.30pm
Trams 13, 14 or 17
The Tandoor F
An Amsterdam institution, the first Indian restaurant in the city and still popular for inexpensive tandoori dishes, plus views over the busy nightlife of Leidseplein.
Leidseplein 19 (tel: 623 4415)
Open: daily 5pm–11pm
Trams 1, 2, 5, 6, 7 or 10
Sheesh Mahal F
Good Indian food in ample proportions and excellent homemade *kulfi* ice cream.
Hartenstraat 17 (tel: 626 9607)
Open: daily 5pm–midnight
Trams 13, 14 or 17

INDONESIAN
Amsterdam has numerous Indonesian restaurants, thanks to its colonial legacy, and Amsterdammers love this spicy cuisine as the antithesis to their own bland cooking. By far the majority of the

Eating the Greek way

Cilubang Indonesian restaurant

restaurants serve a hybrid mixture of Indo-Chinese food, often further modified to appeal to Dutch taste. Far more authentic are the specialist restaurants listed below, often family run and serving traditional regional dishes. Most offer a range of *rijsttafels* – set menus consisting of 15 to 45 different dishes served with rice and fiery chilli sauce called *sambal*, best treated with caution. A simple *rijsttafel* of 15 dishes will provide a remarkably cheap meal of varying flavours and textures, while the more expensive versions usually feature a greater range of meat dishes – saté, beef randang, suckling pig, sweet and sour pork and mild curried chicken are typical.

Cilubang F to FFF

One of Amsterdam's best small

Indonesian restaurants, a quiet and relaxing hideaway.
Runstraat 10 (tel: 626 9755)
Open: daily 5pm–11pm
Trams 1, 2, 5, 13, 14 or 17

Orient FF

A good choice for those not familiar with Indonesian cuisine. The helpful menu explains the various dishes that make up a traditional *rijsttafel* banquet. The Wednesday self-service buffet is a popular and inexpensive way of sampling the complete range.
Van Baerlestraat 21 (tel: 673 9428)
Open: daily 5pm–9.15pm
Tram 10

Indonesia F to FFF

Large restaurant specialising in Balinese cuisine with elegant decor, waiters in traditional dress and taped gamalan music in the background.
Singel 550 (tel: 623 2035)
Open: 5pm–11pm
Trams 4, 9, 16, 24 or 25

Sama Sebo FF

Some of the best Indonesian food in Amsterdam. The first evening sitting (6pm) is popular with people going to the theatre or the Concertgebouw but is best avoided in favour of the second sitting (8pm) if you want to linger over your meal.
P C Hooftstraat 27 (tel: 662 8146)
Open: daily 12 noon–1.45pm and 6pm–9.45pm; booking essential
Trams 2, 3, 5 or 12

Speciaal FF to FFF

A semi-tropical gourmet paradise tucked away in the Jordaan district with a loyal band of regular patrons who maintain that this is Amsterdam's best.
Nieuwe Leliestraat 142 (tel: 624 9706)
Open: daily 5.30pm–11.30pm; booking advised
Trams 10, 13, 14 or 17

IRISH
Paddy's Irish Kitchen FF
Traditional dishes, such as Irish stew, transformed into culinary specials. A good choice for inexpensive oysters in season.
Herenstraat 14 (tel: 624 2229)
Open: daily 6pm–11.30pm
Trams 13, 14 or 17

ITALIAN
Casa da David F
Home-made pasta with inventive sauces and first-rate pizza cooked in a wood-fired oven.
Singel 426 (tel: 624 5093)
Open: daily 5pm–11pm
Trams 1, 2 or 5
Mirafiori FFF
All the classic Italian dishes in an elegant setting.
Hobbemastraat 2 (tel: 662 3013)
Open: Wednesday to Monday 12 noon–3pm and 5pm–9.30pm
Pico Bello F
Inexpensive and authentic trattoria, happy to serve a simple pizza or a full meal.
Spuistraat 1D (tel: 627 1282)
Open: daily 5pm–11pm
Trams 1, 2 or 5

JAPANESE
Teppan-Yaki/Yamazato FFFF
Two restaurants staffed by Japanese chefs who perform publicly with enormous style and confidence, using ingredients flown in fresh from Japan daily. Reasonably priced set lunch menus.
Okura Hotel, Ferdinand Bolstraat 333 (tel: 678 7111)
Open: Monday to Friday 12 noon–2.30pm, daily 6.30pm–10.30pm; jacket and tie
Tram 12

MEXICAN
Popocatepetl FF
Youthful and lively restaurant staffed by friendly student waiters. Top-class margeritas and refreshing Mexican beer served in a champagne ice bucket with a wodge of lime in the bottle neck. All the standard Mexican dishes plus popular spare ribs with chunky fried chips.
Nieuwezijds Voorburgwal 163–165 (tel: 662 4541)
Open: daily 5pm–midnight
Tram 3

Viva Mexico

SPANISH
Iberia F
Authentic tapas, paella and zarzuela (fish stew) plus flamenco music.
Hoogte Kadijksplein 16 (tel: 622 3050)
Open: daily 11am–11pm
Trams 4, 9, 16, 24 or 25

SURINAMESE
Marowijn F
Neighbourhood restaurant favoured by local Surinamese, a good place to try this hybrid cuisine which combines

Indonesian-influenced dishes
(introduced by Dutch civil servants)
based on rice and noodles, with South
American dishes based on cassava and
coconut.
Albert Cuypstraat 68–70 (tel: 662 4845)
Open: daily 12 noon–10pm
Trams 4, 24 or 25

SWISS
Bern F
Simple brown café specialising in fondue
and peppered steaks.
Nieuwmarkt 9 (tel: 622 0034)
Open: daily 4pm–1am
Metro station Nieumarkt

THAI
Lana Thai FF
The best in town with a comprehensive
menu.
Warmoesstraat 10 (tel: 624 2179)
Open: Wednesday to Monday 6pm–
11.30pm
Trams 4, 9, 16, 24 or 25

VEGETARIAN
All the restaurants listed above serve
vegetarian dishes, either as part of the
menu or on request. If, however, you
have special dietary preferences, try one
of the following.
Baldur F
Nouvelle cuisine-style organic, vegan
and lacto-ovo dishes. Outdoor dining in
summer.
Weteringschans 76 (tel: 624 4672)
Open: Monday to Saturday 5pm–9pm.
No credit cards or alcohol
Trams 6, 7, 10, 16, 24 or 25
De Waaghals F
Organically produced food and wine and
vegan dishes. Other dietary requirements
catered for if you phone in advance.
Frans Halsstraat 29 (tel: 679 9609)

Open: Tuesday to Saturday 5.30pm–9pm.
No credit cards. No smoking area.
Trams 16, 24 or 25

Amsterdam provides well for the vegetarian
visitor. The Baldur creates nouvelle cuisine,
vegetarian-style

Brown Cafés

The *bruin kroegen,* or brown cafés, of Amsterdam are a uniquely Dutch institution. The typical features are wood-panelled walls and coffee-coloured ceilings, looking as if they had been stained by centuries of tobacco smoke. The wooden tables are sometimes covered in faded Persian rugs to soak up the spilt beer. Brown cafés are an alternative living room, home from home for the regular clientele, a warm place of refuge in winter when the big, pot-bellied stoves are lit and glowing, and the focus of much community activity. People come here for breakfast, morning coffee or an inexpensive lunch, to relax after work, read the paper, play chess, snooker or draughts or just to chat with their friends.

Brown cafés are found on every street corner, but many of the most characterful are in the Jordaan district. Café 't Smalle *(Egelantiersgracht 12; trams 10, 13, 14 or 17)* is one of the oldest, originally founded in 1780 as the outlet of a gin distillery; it retains its 18th-century interior and stained glass windows and serves spicy Dutch apple cake to help soak up the beer.

On Spui *(trams 1, 2, 4, 5, 9, 14,* *16, 24 or 25)* you will find three very popular cafés within a short distance of each other. Café **Hoppe** *(Spui 18–20),* with its sawdust-covered floor, was founded in 1670 and is popular with trendy business executives, while **Luxembourg** *(Spui 22)* is favoured by university academics and **De Zwarte** *(Spuistraat 334)* is the haunt of artists and journalists; the distinctions often blur in summer when the cafés spill out on to the pavements to form one happy throng.

A variation on the brown café is the *proeflokaal,* or tasting house, where you can sample a very wide range of different beers, wines, gins or liqueurs. One of the most atmospheric is Wijnand Fockink, tucked away off Dam square at *Pijlsteeg 31 (trams 1, 2, 5, 13, 14 or 17).* A more recent phenomenon is the so-called white café – designer bars with high-tech interiors – such as Oblomow *(Reguliersdwarsstraat 40; trams 4, 9 or 14).* White is, however, too clinical a colour for the taste of many Amsterdammers who only feel really at home surrounded by the mellow patina of aged wood and the golden colours of a Rembrandt painting.

The atmosphere in a brown café is anything but dull

A welcome sign for beer-drinkers

Good times in a brown café

Hotel Tips

Although Amsterdam has a great number of hotels, it is also a popular tourist destination and has a thriving conference trade so advance booking is essential in the busiest seasons – Christmas and New Year, Easter and from the beginning of the bulb season in late March to the end of summer, mid-September.

The welcoming Park Hotel

One of the simplest ways to book accommodation is to use The Netherlands Reservation Centre (National Reserverings Centrum), PO Box 404, 2260 AK Leidschendam, *(tel: 070 320 2500 or fax: 070 320 2611)*; open Monday to Friday 8am–8pm, Saturday 8am–2pm. (Reservations can be made in writing, by telephone or fax – no personal callers.) This free service covers the whole of the country and will save numerous potentially fruitless phone calls to individual hotels. The Centre publishes a useful guide called *Hotels in Holland,* available from the Centre, from local VVV Tourist Information Centres and from overseas branches of The Netherlands Tourist Authority.

Hotels in The Netherlands are graded according to a star system, from the cheapest one-star establishments to five-star elegance. As with all such systems, the classification is a useful guide to price and facilities but tells you nothing about the character of the hotels and their owners.

In Amsterdam, the choice essentially falls into three categories: canal-side hotels (price range from F135 to F185 for a double bedroom), family-run hotels (price range from F100 to F150) and larger establishments (F165 upwards). For most visitors, the idea of a centrally located hotel within the canal circle is very appealing. The main drawback is that these buildings are often protected monuments so the owners cannot simply instal lifts, enlarge the rooms or put in modern facilities at will. Rooms may be small and the staircases are often as steep as ladders, so the less-mobile visitor will have real problems. On the plus side, many canal-side hotels have attractive gardens and retain characterful period details, redolent of the Golden Age; their proud owners also ensure that the rooms are appropriately furnished with antiques. There are also many elegant purpose-built hotels in the Dam square and station area which combine the benefits of centrality with a much greater range of facilities.

Most of the family-run hotels in Amsterdam are located in the Museum Quarter and Vondelpark district. Visitors must be sure to check the precise location before booking; do not trust descriptions that say '10 minutes from the centre'. Hotels in the streets immediately around the three big museums make an ideal base, but the further out you go into the Vondelpark district, the more remote you are from public transport and the further it is to walk to the main sights of interest. Family-run hotels offer clean basic accommodation at reasonable prices. As with all but the most expensive hotels, breakfast is included in the room price, but too many hotels serve an unappetising buffet of processed cheese, cheap cooked meats, tasteless bread and lukewarm tea or coffee. Any hotel that offers a better choice is to be preferred.

The larger hotel establishments are dotted all over the city and they range from palatial Empire-style buildings with grand staircases and spacious balconied

The Hotel Barbizon

rooms, to ultra-modern buildings with waterfalls, art galleries and huge atriums. They all have the facilities you would expect of an international-class hotel – business centres, pools and fitness centres, shopping, valet parking and hairdressers.

If you are visiting Amsterdam on business, it may be worth sacrificing a central location for the greater convenience of a modern hotel on the edge of the city. The problems of driving and parking in Amsterdam are such that busy business executives do not like coming into the centre if they can avoid it. Most industry is located on the southern periphery and some of the best hotels are to be found in the same area, close to the RAI exhibition centre and World Trade Centre. Your Dutch counterparts will thank you for choosing a hotel where they can park easily and you are only a short taxi ride from the nightlife of the city centre.

The Hotel Pulitzer

Practical Guide

ARRIVING
Passports
All visitors must have a valid passport to visit The Netherlands but visas are only required if your stay exceeds three months.

Getting There
Amsterdam is easily reached by ferry from the United Kingdom, by train from continental Europe and by road from west Germany, Belgium and northern France. Even so, most visitors arrive by air, flying into Schiphol international airport, located 14km southwest of the city centre. This is one of the world's best and busiest airports, served by direct flights from most other international airports. Competition on these routes is such that you can nearly always find an inexpensive flight if you book far enough in advance and travel midweek.

Airport facilities
Schiphol is very efficient and you should clear the airport within 20 to 30 minutes of landing. There is a bureau de change in the arrivals hall as well as duty-free shopping, an accommodation booking desk and car rental facilities.

City link
The escalator to Schiphol station is right opposite the customs exit. Trains depart from platform *(Spoor)* 1 every 15 minutes from 6am to midnight and at hourly intervals through the night. The fare is inexpensive and the journey takes 20 minutes. Be sure to catch a train for Amsterdam CS (Centraal Station) if you are staying in the city centre. Do not board trains for Amsterdam Zuid or Amsterdam RAI unless you are staying in the World Trade Centre/RAI exhibition centre district in the southern suburbs. On arrival in Amsterdam it is best to take a taxi from the station to the

Nieuwmarkt metro station

Schiphol airport

hotel until you have gained your bearings.

Departing

Remember to confirm your flight with the issuing airline 72 hours before departure (airline telephone numbers are listed in the Amsterdam *Yellow Pages* directory). Check-in time at Schiphol is two hours before the scheduled flight time. There are excellent shopping and duty free facilities at the airport – seeds, bulbs and floral bouquets are popular purchases but some countries do not allow the import of plant material; the knowledgeable florists will advise you.

By train, ferry or coach

There are good, fast rail connections to Amsterdam from Brussels, Paris, Antwerp and Cologne. From London, boat/train services operate from Liverpool Street staion via the Hook of Holland and from Victoria via Dover and Ostend. Ferry companies in the UK offer services from Harwich to the Hook of Holland, from Hull to Rotterdam and from Sheerness to Vlissingen, with train connections from each ferry terminal to Amsterdam. Coach services depart from London's Victoria coach terminal. Details of all these services are available from Thomas Cook and other travel agents but remember that the journey time can be anything from 7 to 14 hours and that it is often just as cheap to fly.

CAMPING

The best-equipped and most central campsite is located on the southern edge of the Amsterdamse Bos, at *Kleine Noordijk 1 (tel: 641 6868)*. Using bus 171 or 172 it is a 30-minute journey to the city centre. Facilities include telephones, a shop, restaurant and bar, bicycles for hire and log cabins for rent equipped with cookers and beds.

CHILDREN

Children are generally welcomed and indulged. Many restaurants offer children's menus *(kindermenu)* or children's portions at reduced prices. Children also pay reduced fares on public transport.

Museums admit infants for free and,

Wheel life in Amsterdam

as a rule, children under 16 are admitted half price. Several museums offer discounted family tickets (two children and two adults), but the best deal for anyone planning to visit several museums is the Museumcard.

CLIMATE

Amsterdam has a maritime climate so it rarely suffers temperature extremes. It is only cold enough for long enough to freeze the canals once in every 10 to 15 years, though it can seem cold in winter because strong winds increase the chill factor, and fog can blot out the sunlight for days on end. Summer temperatures average 22°C/77°F, but it will be warmer during the day and the nights will often be cool enough to make a light sweater necessary. It can rain at any time but prolonged heavy rain is only a problem in November, February and March.

Weather Chart Conversion
25.4mm = 1 inch
°F = 1.8 × °C + 32

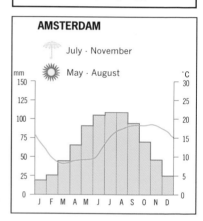

Children welcome almost everywhere

CONVERSION TABLE

FROM	TO	MULTIPLY BY
Inches	Centimetres	2.54
Centimetres	Inches	0.3937
Feet	Metres	0.3048
Metres	Feet	3.2810
Yards	Metres	0.9144
Metres	Yards	1.0940
Miles	Kilometres	1.6090
Kilometres	Miles	0.6214
Acres	Hectares	0.4047
Hectares	Acres	2.4710
Gallons	Litres	4.5460
Litres	Gallons	0.2200
Ounces	Grams	28.35
Grams	Ounces	0.0353
Pounds	Grams	453.6
Grams	Pounds	0.0022
Pounds	Kilograms	0.4536
Kilograms	Pounds	2.205
Tons	Tonnes	1.0160
Tonnes	Tons	0.9842

Men's Suits

UK	36 38 40 42 44 46 48
Rest of Europe	46 48 50 52 54 56 58
US	36 38 40 42 44 46 48

Clothes shoppers will find that Amsterdam caters to most tastes, from the chic and elegant to the young and casual

Dress Sizes

UK	8 10 12 14 16 18
France	36 38 40 42 44 46
Italy	38 40 42 44 46 48
Rest of Europe	34 36 38 40 42 44
US	6 8 10 12 14 16

Men's Shirts

UK	14 14.5 15 15.5 16 16.5 17
Rest of Europe	36 37 38 39/40 41 42 43
US	14 14.5 15 15.5 16 16.5 17

Men's Shoes

UK	7 7.5 8.5 9.5 10.5 11
Rest of Europe	41 42 43 44 45 46
US	8 8.5 9.5 10.5 11.5 12

Women's Shoes

UK	4.5 5 5.5 6 6.5 7
Rest of Europe	38 38 39 39 40 41
US	6 6.5 7 7.5 8 8.5

CRIME

Amsterdam's crime problem has been greatly exaggerated and the situation is improving. Visitors are no more likely to be robbed here than in London or any big American city. Even so, it is essential to take precautions – most victims of crime invite trouble by carelessness or ill-advised behaviour. Highly organised teams of pickpockets, mainly from North Africa and South America, operate in summer, preying on tourists who are silly enough to carry their valuables in a shoulder bag or easily accessible pocket. Leave valuables in the hotel safe and if you must carry them, conceal them in a body belt or similar and keep a tight hold on your camera. Be especially wary in crowded shopping streets or on public transport. Beware of anyone who approaches you, no matter how harmless their enquiry; they may be distracting your attention while an accomplice goes to work. You should also be careful when giving money to buskers or beggars; there are people about watching to see where you keep your money.

After pickpocketing, car theft is the biggest category of crime. Never leave valuables in the car.

Mugging is less of a problem, but do not go out alone after dark anywhere where drug addicts, desperate for a fix, could attack you unseen; avoid parks, unlit and empty streets and the red light district – and never try to take photographs in the red light district; your camera could end up in the canal.

If you are the victim of crime, you should file a statement with the nearest police station; it is unlikely that your property will be recovered, but you need an officially stamped copy of the statement form to make an insurance claim.

Report the loss of your passport to your embassy or consulate (see below). Lost or stolen credit cards can be reported on the following 24-hour lines:
American Express *642 4488*
Diner's Club *627 9310*
MasterCard *010 457 0887*
Visa *520 5534*
Lost or stolen Thomas Cook travellers' cheques should be reported on *06 022 8630 (freephone)*. The Thomas Cook bureaux listed on p183 can give emergency assistance.

CUSTOM REGULATIONS

Personal possessions are not liable to duty but it is forbidden to import drugs, firearms or weapons (including knives). The current duty-free limits for the import of alcohol, tobacco and toiletries are posted at airports and ferry terminals, but these are about to be superceded by new allowances so generous that it is unlikely any ordinary traveller will exceed them.

All possessions should be made safe and secure

CYCLING

Cycling in Amsterdam takes practice and courage, and the excellent tram system offers a far easier way of getting around. You may, however, wish to escape the city and explore nearby nature reserves (see Cycle Routes in Away from it all). The main places for renting a bike in Amsterdam are as follows:

MacBike, *Marnixstraat 220 (tel: 626 6964), tram 1, 2, 5, 10, 13 or 17; and at Nieuwe Uilenburgerstraat 116 (tel: 620 0985), tram 9, 14 or Waterlooplein Metro.*

Koenders Take a Bike, *Amsterdam Centraal station, Stationsplein 6 (tel: 624 8391)*

Damstraat Rent a Bike, *Pieter Jacobszdwarsstraat 11 (tel: 625 5029), tram 4, 9, 14, 16, 24 or 25.*

To hire a bike you need to leave a deposit and show your passport or a credit card. It is best to hire a bike with conventional brakes and gearing: old-fashioned Dutch bikes have no gears or hand brakes and are stopped by back pedalling. You will be given advice on how to avoid theft, which should be heeded. You will then have to cope with chaotic traffic and the wayward behaviour of pedestrians and other cyclists. As a good tip, it is best to dismount at busy junctions and cross on foot until you have mastered the basic rules.

DISABLED TRAVELLERS

Steep hotel staircases and broken pavements are the main hazards facing disabled travellers. Otherwise Amsterdam has an enlightened policy towards people with special needs and most museums, cinemas and theatres have wheelchair access and adapted toilets. Brochures issued by The Netherlands Board of Tourism and VVV

Trams are part of the landscape

Tourist Information Centres include details of hotels and tourist attractions with access and facilities for the disabled. You can also obtain a summary leaflet entitled *Holland for the Handicapped.*

Trams are impossible to use with a wheelchair because of high steps but there are lifts in all Metro stations, except for Waterlooplein, and there is a special taxi service for wheelchair users *(tel: 613 4134, office hours Monday to Friday 9am–6pm, advance booking essential).*

In Amsterdam you can obtain information or report a problem you think needs addressing by contacting the English-speaking staff of Gehandicaptenoverleg *(Keizersgracht 523, tel: 638 3838, open Monday to Friday 9am to 5pm)*, an organisation that works to improve facilities for the disabled in the city.

DRIVING

Driving in Amsterdam is not recommended. The city already has too many cars, parking is difficult, wheelclamp operators very vigilant and cars are a favourite target of thieves. If you do choose to drive to Amsterdam, choose a hotel with secure parking facilities and leave your vehicle there for the duration of your stay.

Cars in traffic

Breakdown

If you are a member of an overseas motoring association you can use the services of the ANWB (Royal Dutch Touring Club) for free on production of a membership card or documents. For the emergency breakdown service, tel: 060 888. If you are not covered by this scheme it may be worth joining the ANWB for the duration of your stay: office at *Museumplein 5 (tel: 673 0844), open Monday to Friday 8.45am– 4.45pm, Saturday 8.45am–12 noon.*

Car Rental

Drivers over 21 with at least a year's experience can hire a car on production of a valid licence, passport and credit card. The main rental agencies *(auto*

verhuur) all have offices at Schiphol airport and at the following city-centre addresses:
Avis, *Nassaukade 380 (tel: 683 6061)*
Budget Rent a Car, Overtoom 121 (tel: 612 6066)
Europcar, *Overtoom 51–53 (tel: 618 4595)*
Hertz, *Overtoom 333 (tel: 612 2441)*

Thomas Cook bureaux in the city also sell car rental.

Slightly less expensive are the following local firms:
Adam's, *Nassaukade 344–347 (tel: 685 0111)*
Kasper & Lotte, *Van Ostadestraat (tel: 671 0733).*

Chauffeur-Driven Cars

Avis, *Nassaukade 380 (tel: 683 6061)*
Doelen Limousine, *Schakelstraat 13 (tel: 682 3151)*

Documents

To enter The Netherlands with a car you need to carry the vehicle registration documents, proof of insurance (eg a Green Card), proof that the vehicle is roadworthy (eg an MOT certificate) and your driving licence. You must also affix an international identification disc to the rear of the car. If you belong to a motoring organisation, bring your membership card or documents to make use of the AWNB breakdown services for free (see **Breakdown**).

Rules of the Road

Traffic drives on the right. Front seat belts must be worn and rear seat belts if fitted. It is illegal to drive after drinking any amount of alcohol. Maximum speeds are 120kmh on motorways, 80kmh on main roads and 50kmh in built-up areas. Many residential areas have adopted traffic-calming schemes and laid down 'sleeping policemen', raised ridges in the road; they are identified by a sign showing a white house against a blue background and in these zones it is illegal to drive faster than walking pace.

Parking

Apart from hotels, secure parking is available at Europarking, *Marnixstraat 250 (tel: 623 6664)*. Metered parking is available along the banks of the main canals but spaces are difficult to find during office hours. Your car is very likely to be clamped if you outstay the allotted time shown on the meter; in this case the ticket affixed to the window will explain where and how to pay your fine. Cars parked illegally or dangerously will be removed to the police car-pound and will only be released after the payment of a substantial fine in cash. The pound is next to Centraal station at Oostelijke Handelskade 2; information from the traffic police, *tel: 627 5866.*

Petrol

Twenty-four hour petrol stations *(benzinestation)* are located at *Marnixstraat 250 and Sarphatistraat 225.*

ELECTRICITY

220 volts, continental 2-pin round style plugs. Non-continental appliances will need an adaptor.

EMBASSIES AND CONSULATES

Most are located in Den Haag (The Hague); a comprehensive listing is given in the Amsterdam *Yellow Pages* directory.
Australia, *Carnegielaan 14, Den Haag (tel: 070 310 8200)*
Canada, *Sophialaan 7, Den Haag*
(tel: 070 361 4111)
Ireland, *Dr Kuyperstraat 9, Den Haag (tel: 070 363 0993)*
New Zealand, *Mauritskade 25, Den Haag (tel: 070 346 9324)*
UK, *Koningslaan 44, Amsterdam (tel: 676 4343)*
USA, *Museumplein 19, Amsterdam (tel: 664 5661).*

EMERGENCY TELEPHONE NUMBERS

Police: 622 2222
Fire and ambulance: 06 11
Tourist Medical and Dental Service: 673 7567
Car breakdown: 060 888
Thomas Cook travellers' cheque loss or theft: see p178

Feeding the parking ticket meter

HEALTH

If you need medical or dental treatment, call the Tourist Medical Service on *673 7567*. This 24-hour line is specifically geared to visitors and will refer you to an appropriate doctor, dentist, pharmacy or hospital. You will be expected to pay for treatment so it is wise to take out travel insurance that includes medical cover.

European Community citizens can obtain a partial refund of medical and dental charges by completing form E111, in advance of their visit, from social security offices and some post offices. The form explains how to obtain a refund but the procedure is time-consuming and bureaucratic; in practice it can be simpler to make an insurance claim.

LANGUAGE

English is rapidly becoming the first language of Amsterdam and virtually everyone speaks it fluently. Signs are written in English and Dutch, and menus are printed in several languages, so communication is rarely a problem.

A pleasant promise on a city wall

LOST PROPERTY

For items lost on trains:
NS Lost Property Information, *Stationsplein 15 (tel: 6559 8005), open Monday to Saturday 24 hours, Sunday 7am–10pm.*

For items lost on the bus, tram or Metro system:
GVB Lost Property, *Prins Hendrikkade 108–114 (tel: 551 4911), open Monday to Friday 9am–4pm.*

Otherwise try Police Lost Property, *Waterlooplein 11 (tel: 5595 8005), open Monday to Friday 11am–3.30pm.*

MAPS

Falkplan publishes a series of comprehensive and up-to-date maps in various formats: foldout, pocket book and a 'patent folded' version which is almost impossible to use in windy weather. These and other maps can be purchased at bookshops and the VVV Tourist Information Centre. Free maps are available from Thomas Cook Bureaux.

MEDIA

If your hotel is linked into the cable network you can watch a wide range of TV programmes from all over Europe, including BBC1 and BBC2, French, German, Belgian and Italian stations, children's channels, non-stop pop videos and American news channels. Cable radio supplies BBC Radio 4, the BBC World Service and Voice of America.

Foreign newspapers and magazines are widely available on the day of publication.

MONEY MATTERS

The Dutch unit of currency is the guilder, often written as F, HFl or DFl (short for florin, the Florentine gold coin that formed a common European currency in the Middle Ages). It is currently indicated internationally by

NLG. Notes come in denominations of F5, F10, F25, F50, F100, F250 and F1,000. There are quite a number of forgeries about, especially of the higher denomination notes: check for the watermark and for the raised area; absence of either indicates a forgery. The guilder is subdivided into 100 cents. Coins come in values of 5, 10, 25, 100, 250 and 500 cents.

Credit cards are accepted just about everywhere for higher value purchases, as are traveller's cheques and Eurocheques. Thomas Cook travellers' cheques can be cashed free of commission charges in Thomas Cook bureaux de change.

Amsterdam has scores of bureaux de change, especially around Dam square and along Damrak. Some may include a substantial commission. Hotels also give you a poor rate.

Thomas Cook bureaux de change are located at:

Dam 23–25
Damrak 1–5 (in the Scandic Crown Hotel)
Leidseplein 31A
Munttoren, Muntplein 12A
Van Baerlestraat 40 (full Thomas Cook travel shop services)

All except the last two are open 7 days a week with extended hours in summer, and in addition to cashing travellers' cheques and exchanging currency they sell maps, excursions and car rental, as well as providing help in the event of lost or stolen Thomas Cook travellers' cheques.

Value Added Tax

BTW tax of 18.5 per cent is included in the price of most retail goods so if you are a resident of a country outside the European Community it makes sense to

Street market life

take advantage of the Tax-Free Shopping for Tourists scheme when you make high-value purchases. All participating retailers will give you details of how to obtain a refund.

MUSEUMCARD

Visitors will save a lot of money on museum admission fees by investing in a Museumcard *(Museumjaarkaart)* at the start of their visit. The card may seem expensive but it gives free admission to some 400 museums in The Netherlands, including most of the major museums in Amsterdam. If you make less than 10 museum visits you will probably not recoup the cost but beyond that number you will make considerable savings. The card is valid for the calendar year, but does not admit you to special exhibitions. The card can be obtained from participating museums (eg the Rijksmuseum) or from the VVV Tourist Information Centre, and you need to supply a passport-size photograph.

NATIONAL HOLIDAYS
Businesses and shops are closed on the following days – although many shops now stay open on Good Friday. Museums are open, but for shorter hours, except on Christmas Day and New Year's Day.
New Year's Day (1 January)
Good Friday
Easter Monday
Queen's Birthday (30 April)
Ascension Day
Whit Monday
Christmas Day (25 Decenber)
Boxing Day (26 December).

OPENING HOURS
Banks: normally open 9am to 5pm, though some open until 7pm on Thursday and the GWK Bank in Amsterdam Centraal station never closes.

Shops: many are closed on Monday morning and for one other half day each

A barge on the Oude Schans Canal

week (half-day closing varies from shop to shop and information is posted on the door). Otherwise the core hours are 9.30am to 6pm (5pm on Saturday), with late-night opening until 9pm on Thursday.

ORGANISED TOURS
Boat Tours
Touring the canals of Amsterdam by boat is a must for a different perspective on the city. Tour operators usually supply taped commentaries in several languages to point out the various landmarks along the route. Day cruises last around an hour and there are more expensive lunch and dinner cruises, at which food is served, lasting up to three hours. Cruises depart at roughly 30-minute intervals from 9am to 6pm daily; reservations are required for lunch and dinner cruises, otherwise just turn up at the landing stage. The main operators are:
The Best of Holland, *Amsterdam Centraal station landing stage (tel: 623 1539)*
Rederij Holland International, *Amsterdam Centraal station landing stage (tel: 622 7788)*
Lindenbergh, *Damrak 26 (tel: 622 2766)*
Rondvaarten, *located at the corner of Spui and Rokin (tel: 623 3810)*

Walking Tours
Two organisations offer interesting personalised tours of Amsterdam on foot. Advance booking is essential:
Archivise, *PO Box 14603, 1001 LC Amsterdam (tel: 625 8908)*. Tours tailored to your interests plus a regular programme of architectural tours.
Mee in Mokum, *Hartenstraat 16 (tel: 625 1390)*; Mokum is the Yiddish name for Amsterdam and, roughly

translated, it means 'the place where you feel at home'. Tours are led by knowledgeable insiders, many of whom have lived in the city all their lives. Tours take place daily from Tuesday to Friday and on Sunday starting at 11am and lasting up to three hours.

Coach tours

Scores of operators offer coach excursions to sights within an hour's drive of Amsterdam, notably to the bulb fields and gardens of Lisse, the windmill museum at Zaans Schans, to the IJsselmeer villages of Volendam, Monnickendam and Marken and to the cheese markets at Alkmaar and Gouda. These can be booked at any hotel, through the VVV Tourist Information Centre or through the branches of Thomas Cook listed on p183.

PHARMACIES

Chemists *(drogisterij)* sell all non-prescription drugs, such as aspirin, plus toiletries, personal hygiene products, tampons and condoms. Chemists are only open during normal shopping hours. If you seek medical help and are given a prescription you will have to go to a pharmacy *(apotheek)* for your medicines. These are normally open Monday to Friday 9am–5.30pm. Details of pharmacies open outside these hours are posted in all pharmacy windows and listed in the newspaper, *Het Parool*. You can also phone the Central Medical Service on *664 2111*, for advice.

PLACES OF WORSHIP

Anglican: English Reformed Church (Engelsekerk), *Begijnhof 48 (tel: 624 9665)*
Roman Catholic: St John and St Ursula, *Begijnhof 30 (tel: 622 1918)*

Jewish (Reformed): *Jacob Soetendorpstraat 8 (tel: 642 3562)*
Jewish (Orthodox): *Van de Boechorstraat 26 (tel: 646 0046)*
Muslim: *Kraainnest 125 (tel: 698 2526)*.

POLICE

In emergency, *tel: 622 2222*. Otherwise contact the Hoofdbureau Van Politie (Police Headquarters), *Elandsgracht 117 (tel: 559 9111)* for help or advice.

POSTAL SERVICES

Stamps can be bought at many tobacconists and souvenir shops. The main post office is at *Singel 250–256 (trams 1, 2, 5, 13, 14, 17 or 21);* open Monday to Wednesdsay and Friday 8.30am–6pm, Thursday 8.30am–8pm and Saturday 9am–3pm. Here you will find the full range of postal services, packaging materials on sale and telephone booths.

Poste restante mail should be addressed to the head office as follows: *Poste Restante, Hoofdpostkantoor PTT, Singel 250–256, 1012 SJ Amsterdam, The Netherlands.* You will need your passport as proof of identity to collect poste restante mail.

PUBLIC TRANSPORT

Amsterdam has an excellent public transport system and a free information folder, with map, is available from the GVB (Amsterdam Transport Authority) office on Stationsplein, alongside the Metro entrance. You can also buy tickets here.

The system is integrated in the sense that the same tickets are valid for tram, bus and Metro travel. The simplest way of getting around is to buy a flat fare ticket from the bus or tram driver or from machines at the entrance to the Metro. Alternatively you can buy one-, two- or three-day rover tickets allowing unlimited use of the system.

The alternative is to buy a strip of tickets *(stripkaarten)* sold in multiples of 10 or 15 at the GVB office or tobacconists. These are valid for one hour's travel and you have to stamp one ticket for each zone you travel through, plus one. In practice most visitors are unlikely to travel beyond the Central Zone, so you will usually need to stamp two tickets for the journey. Fold the strip and insert the required number of units into the machines; these are located at the entrance to the Metro system or at the rear entrance doors on trams. On buses the driver will stamp the tickets for you. Within the hour you can transfer to other buses or trams or the Metro so long as you stay within the same zone. If you find yourself at all confused, drivers and other passengers are usually helpful.

Museumboat Service

One of the most pleasant ways of travelling round Amsterdam is the Museumboat service. This departs every 30 minutes daily between 10am and 3.15pm from the landing stage opposite Amsterdam Centraal station and does a complete circuit of the city, calling at the following five stops:

Prinsengracht/Elandsgracht junction for the Anne Frankhuis

Singelgracht, in front of the Rijksmuseum, for the Museum Quarter

Herengracht/Leidsegracht junction for the Bijbels, Fodor, Van Loon, Amsterdam Historisch and Allard Pierson Museums

Amstel/Zwanenburgwal junction for the Willet-Holthuysen, Rembrandthuis and Joods Historisch Museums

Oosterdok/Kattenburgergracht junction for the Tropenmuseum and Kromhout Werfmuseum

You can buy an ordinary ticket which

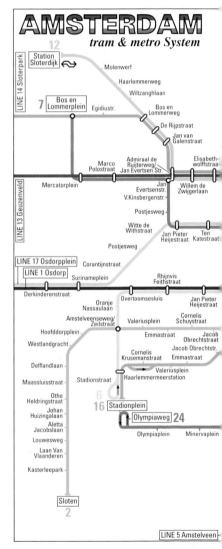

is valid for a day's unlimited use of the service, or a combination ticket whose price includes free entry to three museums at a cost which represents a discount on the normal admission charges. Tickets can be bought from the VVV Tourist Information Centre or at any landing stage.

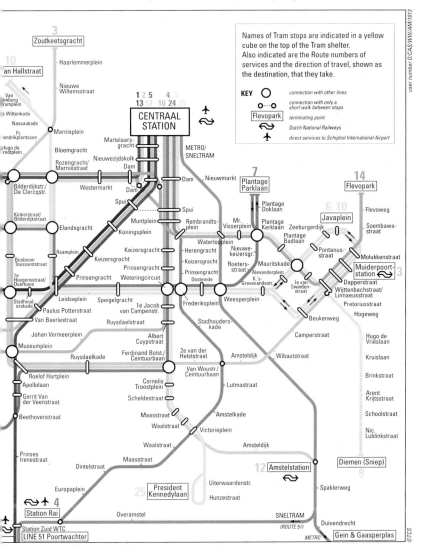

Names of Tram stops are indicated in a yellow cube on the top of the Tram shelter.
Also indicated are the Route numbers of services and the direction of travel, shown as the destination, that they take.

KEY ○   connection with other lines

○--○   connection with only a short walk between stops

Flevopark   terminating point

⇌   Dutch National Railways

✈   direct services to Schiphol International Airport

Taxis

Should you need to use taxis in Amsterdam, you will find the drivers friendly and knowledgeable. You can try hailing a taxi in the street (a lighted sign on the roof indicates that it is free), but it is more usual to go to one of the ranks located on Stationsplein, Dam square, the Museumplein and other well-frequented areas. Alternatively you can call the central taxi reservation number (Taxicentrale), *tel: 677 7777*. The metered fare includes a service charge but it is customary to round the fare up to the nearest guilder.

SENIOR CITIZENS

Pensioners from overseas are entitled to discounted Museumcards (see above) on production of proof of status, but other discounts, on travel for example, are only available to Dutch citizens.

STUDENT AND YOUTH TRAVEL

Students are entitled to discounts on museum entry charges and on Museumcards on production of a valid student identity card or other proof of age or status.

Centraal Station

You can eat very cheaply at one of several large subsidised student canteens (called *mensae*) which anyone can use. The most central is Het Trefcentrum Atrium, *Oudezijds Achterburgwal 237 (tel: 525 3999)*, open Monday to Friday, lunch 12 noon–5pm, dinner 5pm–7pm.

Accommodation in so-called 'youth hostels' is available all over the city at rock bottom prices; you will often be approached by touts as you arrive at Amsterdam Centraal station, and there are plenty of fly posters about advertising their services. They can provide perfectly adequate accommodation but you should check the cleanliness before parting with any money and ensure that your room is not located over a noisy all-night bar or disco. You will be expected to share bedrooms and bathroom facilities with complete strangers so trust nobody and never leave your valuables unattended.

TELEPHONES

In all but the smaller, family-run hotels, IDD telephones are found in every room as a standard facility. The hotel charges a mark up on the normal call rate, so you may prefer to use public facilities for overseas calls.

Public phone boxes are found throughout the city – they have a green livery and carry the green and white PTT Telecom logo. Coin boxes accept F2.5, F1 and 25 cent coins; others are operated by phonecards which can be purchased in various denominations from post offices and phone centres (see below).

To make a call, lift the receiver, wait for the dialling tone and insert your money (25 cents minimum); you will then hear a new higher tone and can dial the number.

Skyline detail above Centraal Station

Codes

For overseas calls first dial *09* and wait for a new tone before dialling the country code.

The code for Amsterdam is *020* – if dialling from abroad omit the initial zero.

International Operator: *06 0410*
International Directory Enquiries: *06 0418*
National Directory Enquiries: *008*

Phone Centres

At the following centres you can make as any calls as you like and pay afterwards with cash, credit card, traveller's cheque or Eurocheque. You can also send faxes and telexes and purchase phonecards:

Telehouse, *Raadhuisstraat 48–50*
(tel: 674 3654)
Open daily 24 hours
Trams 1, 2, 5, 13, 14, 17 or bus 21
Tele Talk Centre, *Leidsestraat 101*

(tel: 620 8599)
Open daily 24 hours
Trams 1, 2 or 5

TIME

Amsterdam observes Central European Time which is one hour ahead of Greenwich Mean Time in winter and two hours ahead from the end of March to the end of September.

TIPS

A service charge is automatically included in the prices on restaurant menus and in metered taxi fares. You may wish to leave a little extra for good service, though this is not obligatory.

TOILETS

Old-fashioned urinals for men are dotted around all over Amsterdam. Women may have to resort to buying a drink in a café in order to make use of their toilets. There are also clean facilities in museums, restaurants and department stores.

TOURIST INFORMATION

The Netherlands has an excellent network of tourist information centres where the standard of service is extremely high. Their official title is Vereniging Voor Vreemdelingenverkeer – the Association for Tourist Traffic – quite a mouthful, hence it is universally abbreviated to the initials VVV (pronounced Vay Vay Vay). Offices are found near the station or main square in every town or city in the country. In Amsterdam the main office is located in a pretty timber building on the waterfront opposite Centraal station *(Stationsplein 10, tel: 626 6444; open Easter to June and September, Monday to Saturday 9am–11pm, Sunday 9am–9pm; July and August daily 9am–11pm; rest of year Monday to Friday 9am–6pm, Saturday 9am–5pm, Sunday 10am–1pm and 2pm–5pm).* This office provides a wide range of services in addition to information and advice; you can use it to book accommodation, entertainment, travel and excursions. It also sells its own

The tradition of blue and white tiles goes back to the early days of their development, when only cobalt was able to resist the firing process

listings magazine, *What's on in Amsterdam,* a range of maps, leaflets, walking and cycling guides and souvenirs and it operates a bureau de change. The branch office at Leidsestraat 106 is open slightly shorter hours and can be used for information and bookings.

Outside the country, branches of The Netherlands Board of Tourism will be found in most capital cities.

A canal stop

ACKNOWLEDGEMENTS

The Automobile Association wishes to thank the following photographers, libraries and museums for their assistance in the preparation of this book.

J ALLAN CASH PHOTOLIBRARY p69
ALL SPORTS p158 (Cor Mooy) p159 (G P Hollande)
AMSTERDAM HISTORICAL MUSEUM p15, 24b, 85c
AMSTERDAM TOURIST OFFICE p4, 13, 86, 176
INTERNATIONAL PHOTOBANK p100, 101
NETHERLANDS BOARD OF TOURISM p11, 12, 57, 70, 72, 118, 120, 122, 163, 176
CHRISTINE OSBORNE PICTURES p67
EDDY POSTHUMA DE BOER p10, 20, 27, 29, 31c, 36, 38a, 43, 45, 49, 50, 51, 52, 53, 54, 56, 60, 61, 62, 64, 65, 71, 74, 75, 82, 83, 87, 88, 89, 91, 94, 96, 97, 97, 100, 103, 104, 105, 106, 107, 109, 111a, 111b, 112, 113a, 113b, 114, 115, 117, 118, 119, 121, 122, 124, 125, 126a, 126b, 128, 129, 130, 134, 135,138, 140, 145a, 145c, 151a 152, 163, 171a, 171c, 174, 183, 188, 189
RIJKMUSEUM FOUNDATION p73, 76, 77, 78/9
REX FEATURES p111
SPECTRUM COLOUR LIBRARY p133
VINCENT VAN GOGH FOUNDATION/VAN GOGH MUSEUM AMSTERDAM p80, 81
W VOYSEY p38b, 38c, 38d, 38e, 55, 63, 67, 68, 89, 92b, 131, 136, 137, 138a, 138b, 138c, 141, 142, 145b, 146, 147, 148, 150, 156, 157, 161, 163, 164, 166, 167, 168, 171b, 172, 173a, 173b, 175, 177, 178, 179, 183, 184, 190b
ZEFA PICTURE LIBRARY p8, 9, 14, 21, 31a, 31b, 63, 98a, 98b, 98c, 102, 116, 127, 160
All the remaining photographs are in the AA Photographic Library, photos taken by Ken Paterson